40

Music Education in
Theory and Practice

The Falmer Press Library on Aesthetic Education

Series Editor: Dr. Peter Abbs, University of Sussex, UK

Setting the Frame

LIVING POWERS:
The Arts in Education
Edited by Peter Abbs

A IS FOR AESTHETIC:
Essays on Creative and Aesthetic
Education
Peter Abbs

THE SYMBOLIC ORDER:
A Contemporary Reader on the
Arts Debate
Edited by Peter Abbs

THE RATIONALITY OF
FEELING:
Understanding the Arts in
Education
David Best

The Individual Studies

FILM AND TELEVISION IN
EDUCATION:
An Aesthetic Approach to the
Moving Image
Robert Watson

LITERATURE AND
EDUCATION:
Encounter and Experience
Edwin Webb

DANCE AS EDUCATION:
Towards a National Dance Culture
Peter Brinson

THE VISUAL ARTS IN
EDUCATION:
Rod Taylor

MUSIC EDUCATION IN
THEORY AND PRACTICE:
Charles Plummeridge

THE ARTS IN THE PRIMARY
SCHOOL:
Glennis Andrews and Rod Taylor

EDUCATION IN DRAMA:
Casting the Dramatic Curriculum
David Hornbrook

Work of Reference

KEY CONCEPTS:
A Guide to Aesthetics, Criticism and the Arts in Education
Trevor Pateman

Music Education in Theory and Practice

Charles Plummeridge

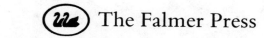 The Falmer Press

(A member of the Taylor & Francis Group)
London • New York • Philadelphia

UK   The Falmer Press, 4 John Street, London WC1N 2ET
USA   The Falmer Press, Taylor & Francis Inc., 1900 Frost Road, Suite 101, Bristol, PA 19007

First published in 1991

A catalogue record for this book is available from the British Library

Library of Congress Cataloging-in-Publication Data are available on request

Jacket design by Benedict Evans

Typeset in 12/14pt Bembo by
Graphicraft Typesetters Ltd., Hong Kong.

Printed in Great Britain by Burgess Science Press, Basingstoke on paper which has a specified pH value on final paper manufacture of not less than 7.5 and is therefore 'acid free'.

Contents

Acknowledgments   *viii*

Series Editor's Preface   *ix*

Introduction   1

Chapter 1   Conceptions of Music Education   7

Chapter 2   Musical Experience and Understanding   25

Chapter 3   The Music Curriculum   45

Chapter 4   Teaching and Learning   67

Chapter 5   Aspects of Evaluation   93

Chapter 6   Music in School and Community   111

Chapter 7   The Teaching of Music: Towards 2000   135

Bibliography   153

Index   163

For Elizabeth Ann

Acknowledgments

I should like to thank Peter Abbs for inviting me to contribute to the Library on Aesthetic Education. His many helpful comments and suggestions on earlier drafts have been greatly appreciated; without his support and encouragement I would never have completed the book.

My colleagues, Keith Swanwick, Dorothy Taylor, John Winter and Mary Scott, have kindly read various chapters and made numerous constructive suggestions; I am most grateful to them for their interest and generous assistance.

I wish to thank colleagues in schools and in particular Gary Firth, Christopher Philpott, Caroline Haines and Mervyn Williams, who have provided valuable information.

Some of the material in Chapter 1 was originally written for The Bedford Way Paper No. 3 *Issues in Music Education*. I wish to thank the Publications Committee of the Institute of Education, University of London for granting permission to reproduce the ideas in this volume.

Preface

'. . . the real function of music begins at a point where
words, intellectually apprehended have no place. Its inherent significance is outside the range of the purely rational
mind. A special exercise of the imagination is needed in
order to recognize a musical idea in a particular series of
sounds, or to recognize in musical ideas a disciplined
expression of deep and obscure human emotions.'[1]

This eloquent passage, so close to the argument in Charles
Plummeridge's *Music Education in Theory and Practice*, comes
from the 1927 edition of the *Handbook of Suggestions* for teachers.
How memorable it is. How different from the leaden formula-
tions that can be found in so many official publications on music
and the arts today. And yet, as Marian Metcalfe made clear in
her historical study of music in the curriculum in *Living Powers*
(the first volume of the Library on Aesthetic Education) music
has seldom been recognized in education for the great symbolic
discipline it is. 'Although music has been included in educational
courses from the earliest time', she claimed, 'it has suffered
more than any of the other arts disciplines in Britain (with the
possible exception of film) from lack of a clear exposition of its
place in both education and community'.[2]

There must be many competing explanations for this failure. Perhaps the most powerful reason lies in the presiding
conception in our long culture of intelligence as verbal, as propositional in nature. *In the beginning was the Word, and the Word*

was with God, and the Word was God.[3] This deep assumption — so deep it is almost never questioned — has promoted verbal forms of understanding at the expense of the non-verbal, at the expense of the spatial, the visual, the kinaesthetic, the musical. It is telling that of the six great art disciplines, literature has always been the most recognized in the English curriculum and has tended to keep itself safely apart from the Arts, often being classified as one of the Humanities. The emphasis on the pro-positional is a major distorting pressure on all the arts which the Aesthetic Library with its commitment to multiple intelligence and aesthetic cognition is committed to shifting. But, as Charles Plummeridge shows in this study, there are other reasons for the comparative neglect of music that can be firmly located *inside* the tradition and theory of music education. Quite simply, many of the models which have been advanced over the last three decades have been deeply inadequate to the full meaning of the subject.

In Chapter 1 Charles Plummeridge analyzes three para-digms of music education and finds them wanting. First, he outlines the traditional model, then the progressive model and, finally, the utilitarian. He sees them as being inadequate in different ways. The traditional model is too prescriptive, the progressive model too child-centred, the utilitarian too narrow — yet they all share two major faults; they fail to grasp the vast symbolic field that constitutes the subject as they also fail to grasp the intrinsic significance of music as a form of knowing. Music education must entail the induction of the student into music; and music consists of all that has been composed, played and responded to, from prehistoric time to the present moment. To teach music is to be responsible to this interactive field of musical expression and, simultaneously, to place the student's innate musical powers firmly within it. To talk only about 'the appreciation of the masters' is both to overlook the child's musical propensities as well as to narrow prematurely the range of possibilities; to talk only of 'self-expression' without reference to the whole symbolic field is to talk, in the end, of a peculiar form of self-deprivation; while to talk only of jobs, utilities and services is to be in danger of missing the great musical point entirely.

That music is an aesthetic field, comparable to while different from the simultaneous order of literature, lies at the heart of Charles Plummeridge's book. To give it a philosophical formulation the author draws on the writings of Paul Hirst, Susanne Langer, Louis Arnaud Reid, John Dewey and Wittgenstein. Examining the latter's theory of language and its implications for music he writes:

> It points to music as being a rule-governed system or a form of discourse. Understanding requires a grasp of musical "grammar" or more precisely "grammars". The grammars will not be learned exclusively through formal educational programmes but their existence does have important implications for curriculum design and practice.

One of the cardinal aims of the teacher must be to bring together the varieties of musical expression within a musically coherent framework. In this insight lies the common ground of the emerging aesthetic pedagogy across the arts, at least as envisaged by the contributors to the Library of Aesthetic Education.

What does it all mean in more practical terms? It means that in the classroom there must be a more comprehensive attention to the structural elements of artistic experience in relationship both to the child's innate musical intelligence and also in relationship to the symbolic field in which the art operates. Charles Plummeridge in this context refers to the practical approach advocated by Keith Swanwick in which music in the classroom is related to three inter-related activities, that of *composition, performance* and *audition* (listening). This is strikingly close to the sequence outlined in *Living Powers*[4] as a model for all the arts. While Plummeridge favours a somewhat more eclectic approach, rightly fearing the restricting consequences of prescriptive models, his final position remains close to that of Keith Swanwick, as also the position of David Hornbrook in *Education in Drama* and Peter Brinson in *Dance As Education*. Animate the symbolic field, would seem to be the cry; and such animation in our polycultural age must, of course, include the artistic work of other cultures as well as that of our own great Western European culture with its endlessly rich and transformative musical tradition. It is not a question of either-or but of both-and. Culturally we cannot afford to be ignorant of our own variegated and often sublime musical tradition, nor can we afford to neglect the challenge and vitality of non-European cultures which are, anyhow, due to the powers of the electronic media, now more and more part of one common musical inheritance.

In this immense expansion of musical content it is important that the student's own individual development does not get, as it were, blocked out or steam-rollered. It is essential that the student enters the musical field *as a creative agent*. Charles Plummeridge is emphatic about the need to work from existing strengths, resources, enthusiasms, both in the teacher and in the student. Teachers of music should never be envisaged as the deliverers of a closed system. An inspiring example of one approach, which brings the creative students and the creative tradition happily together is that given by the teacher and composer Peter Maxwell Davies:

> I take for granted that the teacher will be familiar with rudiments of orchestration, and have a thorough knowledge not only of classical scores, but also of Bartok, Stravinsky, Messiaen, and so on, whom children find particularly stimulating. Having this knowledge, he must paradoxically forget it while dealing with children, otherwise he may still force an adaptation of a solution by Bartok or Stravinsky which the child will apply without further consideration, before having grasped his own problem intensely enough and struggled with his material constructively. Afterwards it is helpful to point out that Beethoven, Bartok or whoever did such and such a thing in a similar circumstance.[5]

In this indirect manner there is great wisdom, for almost unconsciously the student, as a creative being, becomes by degrees a full member of the collective musical culture. Although, as Charles Plummeridge would rightly insist, this too is only one way.

All of this may seem daunting to the music teacher. Yet Charles Plummeridge's book is not daunting. Much of it is written from the viewpoint of an active practitioner and an experienced music-teacher. The author constantly opposes restrictive dogmas and advocates an aesthetic in relationship to actual abilities and actual classroom conditions. He considers also, with great lucidity, many other aspects of music education which I have not so far mentioned: music as a form of knowledge, the problem of musical assessment and evaluation, the demands of the National Curriculum, the place of music in the wider community, the complex double role of the music-teacher, the role of the music-teacher as *Kappelmeister* and the place of music within an arts curriculum.

Now that music has been formally recognized as a foundation subject in the National Curriculum it is structurally possible to provide, for the first time, a comprehensive initiation of every child into the field of music. This is a great and, given the present conditions and constraints, a somewhat daunting task. However, it is a chance that must not be missed. Charles Plummeridge's book will give many music-teachers heart first of all by its recognition of the various methods of teaching music and, secondly, for the framework it offers for their effective integration. It thus provides the conditions necessary for a broad musical education. We must never forget that such an education is the aesthetic birthright of every child born into a democratic culture.

Peter Abbs
Centre for Language, Literature and the Arts in Education
University of Sussex
January 1991

Notes and References

1 Quoted in Marian Metcalfe's 'Towards the Condition of Music' in Abbs, P. (Ed.) *Living Powers: the Arts in Education*, London, Falmer Press, 1987, p. 100.
2 *Ibid.*, p. 97.

3 The opening sentence of the Prologue to *The Gospel According to John.*
4 See *Living Powers, op. cit.*, pp. 52–62.
5 Peter Maxwell Davies 'Music' in BRITTON, J. (Ed.) *The Arts in Education*, George Harrap, 1967, p. 30.

Introduction

It is sometimes said that whenever music teachers are gathered together they always return to discussions of familiar topics. This is probably true. The status of music, its justification as a curriculum subject, the organization of concerts, the various duties of music staff, lack of timetable allocation, inadequate accommodation; all seem to be routine items on the music education agenda. But it is how things should be, for these are central and important professional issues; they will inevitably be of concern to teachers in every type of school. The point is also sometimes made that it is only teachers concerned with so-called weak status subjects who worry about matters such as theories of justification and clarification of aims. This is definitely *not* true. One only has to glance at a few books and documents to realize that those who have some specialist interest in an area of the curriculum are constantly examining and reflecting on the nature and purpose of their work.

Nevertheless, in a system that is dominated by a particular view of knowledge and a tendency to regard education as a means to some extrinsic end, teachers of music often feel under pressure to explain and justify their subject. On occasion, they might find themselves in the position of having to contend with some negative, and even antagonistic, attitudes since arts subjects are frequently regarded as being of only marginal value and significance. There is nothing new about this state of affairs. Numerous official reports on education over many years have recommended that more attention be given to the arts. However, they are still sometimes thought of as peripheral activities. One of the main purposes of this volume is to argue against outdated views which support these attitudes. I want to emphasize the importance of music and the arts within a broad and liberal education, not as optional extras, pastimes, hobbies or forms of relaxation, but as serious and powerful realms of human meaning.

Although the book is written with the music education community in mind it is in no sense 'technical' nor is it a pedagogical manual. Rather, the focus is on what I describe as the background to music teaching. It is therefore to be hoped that the various topics and issues discussed will be of interest to a wider audience. Naturally the views expressed represent a British perspective. Consequently there is frequent reference to a number of domestic concerns such as the National Curriculum and changing patterns of educational provision in this country. However, many of the basic issues have a wider applicability. Indeed, one of the most striking factors to emerge from comparative studies of educational systems is that there are often more similarities than differences between them. This becomes very apparent when working with colleagues from other countries. Music teachers, the world over, seem to have to fight very similar battles. But they also share many of the pleasures and rewards which arise from musical encounters with children and young people.

Whilst the emphasis in this book is on *music* and music education I am very much in accord with those who regard the arts as forms of experience characterized and united by a distinctive perceptual mode of understanding. This is not to view the arts disciplines as being identical or in any way equivalent. There are many differences between them particularly in their procedures, methods and techniques. But to recognize common features, links and similarities does have implications for the organization and teaching of the arts subjects in schools.

I also wish to associate myself with that movement in arts education which emphasizes the significance of tradition and innovation both in music and education. The polarization of traditional and progressive ideals is probably less marked in music education than in some other areas of the curriculum; but from time to time there have been those who have favoured a revolution and an almost complete abandonment of anything which might be seen as preserving the inherited field of musical experience. Most musicians and music teachers have a dislike of extreme positions; they are likely to be suspicious of people who seem to want to deny children access to their cultural inheritance. For musicians the past is far from dead and irrelevant; indeed without it little sense can be made of the present. Many teachers will also reject the views of those confessed music lovers who have little time for music of the twentieth century and others who regard the whole field of popular music as being of no aesthetic import and value. These sorts of exclusive positions can never take us very far in the practice of music education. We live in a society which embraces a rich variety of musical styles and traditions. Educating children in, and for, this society demands that we take cognizance of its multicultural and pluralist character.

Writing about an area of the curriculum at the present time is a slightly risky business because of the rapid changes taking place in education. We never quite know where we are; comments on curriculum policies are often very quickly out of date. However, the issues at the heart of this book are those which have occupied the minds of music educators for several decades and are likely to continue to do so in the foreseeable future. There is a continuous conversation about music education; in this conversation there are many voices expressing a variety of opinions. This book is not intended to be a new conception of music education nor is it a prescription for practice. The ideas explored and developed here are intended to be one small contribution to that wider conversation.

Like many teachers I have always been rather wary of grand theories of education that appear to promise immediate solutions to almost every type of practical problem. All teachers know that education is never straightforward; there is often a big gap between stated intentions and classroom realities. However, underpinning any curriculum action there will be certain beliefs and assumptions about educational aims, worthwhile content and learning processes. These may be described as theoretical positions and will obviously determine practice to some extent. In the opening chapter I critically examine alternative positions in order to illustrate how these lead to specific approaches to music teaching. My own theoretical starting point, and my central thesis, arises from a conception of music as a distinct way of knowing. I develop this idea in Chapter 2 by drawing on various epistemological traditions and psychological theories of intelligence. Discussion of implications for the design and operation of the curriculum arising from this view of music forms the substance of Chapters 3 and 4.

Chapter 5 is devoted to aspects of curriculum evaluation. Here I focus on the study of classrooms, which I regard as being directly linked to the process of curriculum development. It is an important part of my general argument that teachers should be able to utilize different theories not simply for practical guidance but also for the purpose of critical reflection on practice. Curriculum development thus conceived is school and classroom-based; the study of practice yields data which informs decisions about future action. In many ways this style of curriculum development is in marked contrast to the type of thinking and policy associated with the National Curriculum.

There is, of course, a great deal of music making beyond the classroom; most schools have their choirs, orchestras and other ensemble groups. In Chapter 6 I discuss the relationship between class programmes and extracurricular activities. This is a controversial area. There are social, professional and political issues here concerned with the role of the teacher, the scope of school music and patterns of teacher education and training.

In the final chapter I attempt to bring a number of arguments together in order to review current trends and consider future developments in music education. An examination of issues in arts education raises questions not only about curriculum programmes. Inevitably, one is forced to consider education in a broader sense and how education relates to a particular vision of society.

Note

Throughout this book I adopt the policy of using 'he'. This is purely for stylistic reasons and is not intended to imply any gender bias.

Chapter 1

Conceptions of Music Education

Introduction

Some years ago, when I was teaching music in a comprehensive school (and at a time when financial arrangements for INSET provision were very different from what they are now) I was fortunate enough to be seconded for a year to pursue a course in educational studies. On returning to school one of my music department colleagues greeted me in what I recall as a rather strange and slightly hostile manner. We had not seen each other for several months and, ignoring the usual social conventions he simply said, 'don't give me any of that educational theory'. Fortunately, there was no enduring hostility! But this somewhat abrupt reception served to remind one of a commonly held view, namely, that theories of education are often far removed from the practical realities of schools and classrooms. And in some ways there is much to be said in support of such a view. One can talk, read or write about teaching music (or anything else for that matter) but actually *doing* it is a further operation. Suggestions and recommended strategies found in books frequently appear to ignore or neatly avoid the many difficulties and constraints which are part of the daily routine of school life. We have all had the frustrating and disappointing experience of planning lessons and schemes of work which look good on paper but do not have the intended impact when we attempt to translate our plans into what educationists like to call 'effective

7

practice'. To borrow and negate a bit (or rather several bits) of common computer speech, 'WHAT YOU SEE IS OFTEN NOT WHAT YOU GET'.

During the past thirty years or so there has been a substantial increase in theoretical writings on music education. A brief review of the literature reveals a move away from concentration on pedagogical techniques and useful tips to a greater interest in understanding and explaining *musical experience itself* as a necessary prerequisite to the teaching of the subject. There has also been much more detailed examination and clarification of the various ideals and principles that underpin and inform practice. These changes of emphasis owe much to the curriculum development movement of the 1960s. Many members of national project teams concluded that before putting forward proposals for teaching it was necessary to ask some fundamental questions about educational aims, the nature of knowledge and how particular school subjects contributed to pupils' total educational experiences. The Schools Council Project *Arts and the Adolescent*,[1] for example, started out as an attempt to study arts education practices, prior to the production of classroom materials. But it ended up as a 'conceptual framework' designed to assist teachers in re-examining their work and educational role. In an area of the curriculum which has often been neglected and is in need of clearer directions, this theoretical work has been both necessary and valuable. I am well aware of the fact that there are those who would disagree with this interpretation of events and argue that educational theory has in fact clouded practical issues. However, many of the major advances in music education reflect the influence of newly formulated rationales and pedagogical frameworks. Nevertheless, as John Paynter[2] has quite rightly reminded us, it always has to be remembered that whatever guidance may be offered by theorists, researchers, innovators or any other type of curriculum 'expert', it is *teachers* who 'deliver' the curriculum. They have the job of adapting and modifying recommended principles in what are always unique circumstances.

I do not want to labour this point about the uncertain relationship between theory and practice; nor are my remarks intended to support what Keith Swanwick[3] has called a 'fashionable' anti-intellectual and anti-theory stance. But there is a need to distinguish between theory as a prescription for practice and theory as a reflection on practice. Any attempt to prescribe practice in the sense of setting out a blueprint which can be neatly applied to all situations is likely to be strictly limited. The reality of practice is its *particularity*, determined by teachers, pupils, physical conditions, school traditions and many other factors. This is one of the main weaknesses of the National Curriculum — the great theory of our time — and just how far it will ever work remains to be seen. There are many signs of it disintegrating, and the original master plan has been revised on an almost daily basis. This is only to be expected; any curriculum specification is necessarily provisional and bound to change in practice.

Of course, all teachers operate against a background of ideas, beliefs, attitudes and assumptions which may be said to constitute *their* theory or theories, and it is the ability to constantly reflect on this background that is at the heart, not only of curriculum innovation and development, but of all educational practice. Recent legislation has led us to question what we are doing to a greater extent than ever before. There is much more discussion of educational issues and exchange of information amongst staff within schools and Local Authorities. This has led to an increased sense of professionalism and is certainly to be welcomed. The problem with the present reforms, however, is that teachers are being bombarded by new ideas and constantly changing policies to such an extent that many are complaining of 'innovative fatigue' and a feeling of bewilderment. In the end too many rapid changes and innovations could have the effect of stifling educational thinking and imagination. This would obviously be to the detriment of curriculum reform.

I have dwelt on these points because I am anxious to emphasize that this book is not an attempt to outline any sort of ambitious scheme or model for practice. Rather, it is a book of ideas and observations; it represents a style of thinking about education described by Joseph Schwab as the 'Art of the Practical'.[4] The Practical is a way of approaching educational issues which draws on theory for the purpose of deliberation and reflection, not for the formulation of instructions and stated ends. This is not to suggest that in considering educational issues one does not start from some position or theoretical perspective. Indeed, it is impossible to see how things could be otherwise. However, the strength of any position needs to be questioned and tested not only for its internal coherence and validity but also in the light of practice, which is always highly complex and variable.

Two central and closely related themes underpin the ideas developed in this volume. The first is that the six arts — Visual Art, Drama, Dance, Music, Film and Literature — constitute distinct realms of meaning and understanding; these disciplines should feature on the curriculum for all children as an essential part of a liberal education. This proposition is, of course, central to the present library on Aesthetic Education. It is by no means new. But at a time of uncertainty and unprecedented change in the educational system there is a need for further justification and explanation of such a view. Certainly, the notion of liberal education, implicit in the 1944 Act and amplified by educational philosophers and curriculum specialists in the 1960s and 1970s, is in great danger of being brushed aside in favour of more utilitarian considerations and objectives. I want to argue for a reaffirmation of those liberal ideals which lend support to the principle of music and the arts as being *intrinsically* worthwhile, and a meaningful dimension of children's educational experiences. The second main theme, which arises out of the first, is that music is a broad discipline and offers opportunities for a range of experiences. Programmes which focus solely on one particular musical genre or some type of specialized training necessarily restrict and limit experience. Fortunately, we seem to be moving away from extreme and exclusive conceptions of music education (usually advocated by theorists) to more balanced views which find favour with practitioners.

From these two standpoints there are clearly numerous implications for the organization and teaching of music in schools. My intention is not to offer prescriptions or solutions (and certainly not 'tips'). Rather I shall attempt to raise theoretical and practical questions which require various types of critical examination and treatment.

Music Education in Schools

It is well known that although there have been frequent references to musical activities in educational programmes ever since Greek times, opinion has often been sharply divided about their value and significance. Bernarr Rainbow[5] makes the point that whilst some educators have regarded music as a supreme moral force others have condemned it as a thoroughly undesirable and time-wasting pursuit. Consequently, the emergence of the concept of music *education* in the post-war years may be seen as representing a renewed acceptance of a more positive attitude. For to advocate *educating* people in a subject implies that they are to be introduced, through some form of systematic and methodical study, to a valuable and worthwhile area of experience. On this view music would be seen not as a mere relaxation or diversion but as a serious discipline with its own set of meanings as well as its own standards, procedures, skills and techniques.

It would, however, be unwise to assume that there are no longer those who think of music as being anything more than what Cardinal Newman called an 'elegant pastime'. Marian Metcalfe,[6] in *Living Powers*, suggests that such an attitude is not uncommon in our present day society. It may even be found in certain educational circles. For in spite of the fact that music is a foundation subject in the National Curriculum there continues to be a debate about its usefulness and purpose, and although the term music education is now commonly used its meaning is often ambiguous.

This is hardly surprising when one considers the wide range of musical activities in schools. Geoffrey Brace,[7] and others, have drawn attention to a gradual merger of two different traditions of music teaching which has occurred over a fairly long period of time. The maintained schools have inherited the old elementary system of class music teaching, instituted and developed in the nineteenth century by educators such as Sarah Glover and John Curwen. Many schools have also added forms of non-timetabled music making (e.g. choirs and orchestras) which originated in the independent sector and were managed by a 'Director of Music'. This has led to a situation in which the majority of pupils experience music as a class subject at some stage of their school careers, whilst a relative minority participate in so-called extracurricular or voluntary activities. Of course, the organization and provision varies from school to school but the general pattern is familiar to most teachers. Originally the extracurricular work was considered important insofar as it contributed to the style and character of the school community. In a fascinating book covering musical life in Britain during the years 1845–1945, Percy Scholoes[8] provides a number of vivid examples which illustrate the enthusiasm for music at schools such as Uppingham and Harrow in the late nineteenth century. By and large, however, being a member of, say, a school orchestra was regarded as a worthwhile aspect of a pupil's social and cultural experience rather than a significant part of his education. No doubt this attitude still persists in some schools. However, there would seem to be a growing tendency to regard extracurricular activities in music, and other areas, as providing opportunities for both personal and social development. This is seen as an important aspect of a child's total educational experience. At the present time, therefore, music education may be seen as a 'family' of activities, and any full study of the field will have to take account of both timetabled lessons and extracurricular pursuits.

I think it is very important to emphasize this broader view of music education because with the advent of the National Curriculum there may be a tendency to think of music as just another 'school subject'. The fact that it does appear as one of the foundation group is some recognition of its value. If music is to be a potent force in children's education it must (along with the other arts subjects) be given a proper amount of curriculum time. But musical and artistic pursuits also make an important contribution to the general character of schools. They can, and frequently do, permeate the life of an institution in a very special and distinctive way. Anybody working in a school will be aware of how concerts, plays and other 'public' artistic events bring with them the excitement and 'magic' of the arts. This can have an enormous motivational effect on pupils. Through these activities they learn from each other and are often inspired by each other. Commitment to the arts is picked up in all sorts of informal and unplanned ways when pupils are in an environment where artistic pursuits are appreciated and valued. Formalized instruction is obviously an indispensible part of any educational programme, but it would be a great cultural loss if we got so caught up in the technicalities of the new curricula, with the emphasis on the achievement and assessment of specified skills, knowledge and understanding, that these broader aspects of music education were overlooked. Schools are not institutions concerned solely with ensuring that pupils acquire measurable amounts of knowledge and information. They are communities with their own particular styles, traditions and customs. Indeed, without artistic activity schools would become dull and impoverished places; they would lack that sense of identity and social cohesion so essential in any community. I would maintain that most headteachers, school governors, parents and members of the public share this view. They recognize the important contribution the arts make to the overall quality of the educational environment.

Trends and Issues

Over the past fifty years one of the characteristic features of class music teaching in British schools has been its increasing diversity. In a decentralized system where teachers have been largely responsible for the design of their own curricula, it is almost inevitable that there will be different approaches to teaching, choice of activities and the selection of curriculum content. During recent years there have been moves to establish a common framework for music education, often in the belief that this will strengthen both the status and teaching of the subject. The National Curriculum itself is based on the principle that a certain conformity is one of the necessary requirements for curriculum reform and development. But to what extent conformity in practice is feasible (or even desirable) is a complicated issue and dependent on a variety of factors. One important matter that is often not appreciated (or understood), is that curriculum change is evolutionary and relatively slow. Practice does not suddenly conform to a new set of rules and regulations simply because these happen to be written down in documents issued by the Department of Education and Science. Even more important is that, underlying different practices in music teaching, there may well be alternative, and sometimes conflicting, conceptions of education.

Because of the range of practices in our schools it is perhaps tempting to try to identify particular trends which could be classed as 'theories' of music education. We sometimes talk of a 'traditional' approach to music teaching as one which is concerned with choral and instrumental programmes, skill acquisition (particularly literacy skills), 'academic' studies and the appreciation of the works of the great classical masters. Alternatively, there is frequent reference to the 'progressive' ideals of creativity and self-expression to be promoted through experimentation and the exploration of sound materials. The obvious danger of devising educational typologies is that these can become little more than caricatures of existing practices. Amongst any group of educators who might be classed as either traditional or progressive there will be a number of opinions about the place of music in education and how the subject should be presented and taught to pupils. Nevertheless, through an analysis of research findings and relevant literature, it is possible to identify different justifications and rationales which account, at least in some measure, for certain styles of practice. I shall briefly discuss different types of justifications and in so doing attempt to make my own musical and educational perspectives more explicit.

Justifications for Music

There is a popular view of education which can be traced back to the ideals of certain Victorian reformers. On this view the aim of education should be to equip children with skills and knowledge that will enable them to eventually obtain suitable employment and also use their leisure time in a profitable and meaningful way. Music and the arts have frequently been seen as wholesome pursuits which young people can turn to in adult life. Indeed, many of the Victorians regarded musical activity as being morally beneficial and, therefore, a means of bringing about social control and reform. The idea of leisure education, although without the moral tone, is to be found in a document produced by the Incorporated Society of Musicians[9] some forty years ago. It reappears in the Newsom Report[10] and more recently in the writings of Atarah Ben Tovim.[11] 'Conventional' musical activities are justified as part of an education which 'prepares' pupils for the life of work and leisure.

Certainly many pupils do acquire musical interests as a result of their experiences in school, and there will be those who continue to pursue these interests in adulthood. With opportunities in the post-war years for more children to receive instrumental tuition in schools there is every reason to believe that an increasing number of people have found fulfilment through active involvement in music. Teachers and musicians will obviously welcome these developments. But the principle of education for leisure needs closer inspection, for although it implies a worthy aim it also gives rise to a number of distinct problems.

To begin with, it might be argued that since the majority of the adult population is not actively engaged in musical pursuits, in any regular way, music educators have failed to realize their aims. Pupils have not received an adequate education during the formative years; they have not been properly prepared. No doubt there are those who would subscribe to this position just as some would 'blame' schools for football hooliganism and all the other ills of society. But it is a very simple and restricted view. It completely disregards the numerous factors that shape people's lives; many are nothing at all to do with formal education.

The most serious difficulty arising out of the notion of education for leisure is that the meaning of leisure is not clear. The word is used in connection with a range of pastimes and pursuits, but the implication of doing something 'at one's leisure' is that the task in question is not too important and does not require urgent attention. Proponents of leisure education frequently seem to overlook the fact that people who are really committed to some form of music-making often do not regard it as a leisure pursuit at all. I meet and work with many busy amateur musicians who sometimes make the point that they have little or no leisure time. This is because musical activity, if it is to be approached seriously, imposes commitment, discipline, hard work and concentrated effort. Of course, participation in musical pursuits gives great pleasure and satisfaction but it is only leisure in the sense of being separate from employment. For many people it may well be regarded as the most important part of their lives. I would suggest that there are those who actually turn away from music-making largely because it does not conform to what they think of as leisure. In fact people do not involve themselves in artistic activities in order to fill up their spare time. They get involved because they see some *point* in a particular activity, not because they are seeking simple entertainment or a form of relaxation.

Richard Hoggart has commented that much of the debate about educating for leisure sounds rather like aiming 'to keep people docile by providing opiates'.[12] Those who have a routine job (or are retired) are seen as being in need of plenty of leisure opportunities and facilities as a protection against boredom and aimlessness. Much of leisure education does focus on the arts and various craft pursuits, but who is to say how people might use their time when not at work. Why should a person not pursue mathematics or philosophy during 'off duty' hours rather than music, games, drama or flower arranging? It is surely to be hoped that people will develop all sorts of interests as a result of their general education.

One of the most regrettable consequences arising from the idea of preparation for 'work' and 'leisure' is that it reinforces negative attitudes towards the content of the school curriculum. Certain subjects assume central importance because of their connection with vocational preparation. Subjects not in this category are likely to be seen as of only secondary concern. Music and other arts subjects tend to be relegated to the latter group since they are not usually regarded as being essential to future career prospects. Teachers will feel a responsibility in seeing to it that their pupils are properly equipped with skills and knowledge demanded by employers. The arts will be of only minor signifiance. Education, on this view, is simply a means to an end. The educated person is somebody who is in an occupation commensurate with his ability and who engages in 'approved' types of leisure pursuits.

An alternative, and what may be regarded as a more progressive justification, is that music and the arts are directly related to the 'life of feeling'. Any well-balanced system of education should be one that takes into account the development of children's intellectual and feeling capacities. Malcolm Ross[13] and Robert Witkin[14] outlined a convincing view of arts education based on this principle and advocated activities which would promote creative self-expression and pupils 'feeling states'. Witkin's conception of education is based on a psychological account of knowing which draws on, and adapts, the genetic epistemology of Piaget. He distinguishes between 'object knowing' — the individual's knowledge of the world 'out there' — and 'subject knowing' — the knowledge a person has of his 'inner being'. Individuals come to understand their two worlds through the process of adaptation; this involves the development of both types of knowing. For Witkin, education *is* adaptation. He argues strongly that the creative arts have a vital function in relation to subject knowing; it is through making (i.e. creating) art that people 'recall' their feeling and consequently gain further knowledge of their 'being'. Witkin is of the opinion that much educational practice fails to take into account the importance of subject knowing. This is to the impairment of children's development and psychological well-being.

The theoretical and practical difficulties posed by this 'psychological' model of education have been widely debated by arts educators and it would seem unnecessary to review them again here. From the point of view of justification, the biggest problem arising from Witkin's position is the dualistic theory of mind, relating the sciences to the intellectual and the arts to feeling. Louis Arnaud Reid[15] maintains that all knowledge has something of the affective about it; to think of disciplines like Mathematics and Science as 'cold' intellectual forms of inquiry is mistaken. David Best[16] has further argued that such a separation of the cognitive and the affective is not only philosophically untenable but also damaging to the cause of arts education.

Both Ross and Witkin are highly critical of a form of music education which places emphasis on the 'ceremonial use of music' and the 'conservation of the cultural heritage'. What they fail to appreciate is that in schools, groups such as choirs and orchestras have a role in the school community just as orchestras, brass bands and male voice choirs do in a town or village. Such musical groups add something to the quality of everybody's lives; they are not solely for the enjoyment and satisfaction of the participants. They reflect the life of communal feeling in a very real sense. It also needs to be remembered that through our cultural inheritance we gain a unity that gives meaning to both self and society. We may not wish to recommend a curriculum based entirely on the works of the great masters, folk songs or hymn tunes, but these are of musical and aesthetic value. They are part of that symbolic order which constitutes society. There does seem to be something a bit odd in saying, on the one hand that education involves adapting to the environment, whilst on the other that the cultural heritage has no place in a dynamic arts curriculum. The cultural *inheritance* is very much part of the environment; it is part of the cultural continuum.

In making these critical comments I am not wishing to suggest that the two types of justification considered above are not without some merit. But what I think is limited about both of them is that neither pays sufficient attention to the strong conceptual connection between education and intrinsically worthwhile activities. However, in a sense this connection is unwittingly pre-supposed. The fact that people commend music and arts activities as suitable for leisure education, rather than pursuits like horse racing and simple card games, would indicate that within an *educational* context some activities are regarded as more worthwhile than others. It could be argued that preparing children for leisure pursuits is just another way of introducing them to worthwhile activities. The same sort of argument might equally apply to the notion of education as adaptation with its emphasis on the importance of developing the life of feeling. It makes no sense to talk of feeling as some independent mental operation. We feel *about* things and as educators we direct pupils to things which we consider *worth* feeling about.

This conception of education as being concerned with introducing pupils to (or 'initiating' them into) worthwhile activities owes much to the seminal writings of Professor Richard Peters.[17] Central to this view is the principle of education as development of *mind* through the acquisition and understanding of knowledge. Traditionally, the arts have not been regarded as knowledge. Therefore their place in education, if they have had a place at all, has been seen as being of little importance. But there is a new awareness of the arts as forms of meaning and knowing, and a revival of views which have been overshadowed by the dominance of scientific and positivist schools of thought. In fact, the idea that music may be regarded as a way of knowing, rather than a pleasurable auditory sensation (or 'innocent luxury' as Dr. Burney put it) actually has a long history. Paul Hindemith,[18] in seeking to explore the question of musical values turns, perhaps rather surprisingly, to the writings of Roman philosophers; he is particularly influenced by the works of St. Augustine. Hindemith draws on Augustine's notion of music as a generator of moral power resulting from active mental participation in, and with, music. This leads Hindemith to conclude that the eternal and lasting values in music are not to be found in musical works themselves. Musical values exist in that form of *mental activity* which converts sounds or acoustic effects into meaningful structures. Music has a *cognitive* dimension. In more modern times the view of music as a form of knowing has been reasserted and further developed by philosophers such as Suzanne Langer, Philip Phenix and Louis Arnaud Reid. It would be quite wrong, of course, to assume that these philosophers share an identical epistemology, but they all regard knowledge as being far more than that which can be set out in the form of verifiable statements or propositions. This newer conception of knowledge is central to my own view of music education and I shall explore it further in the following chapter.

Some Conclusions

During the past ten years or so we have witnessed what appears to be an attempt to reconcile so-called traditional and progressive approaches to the teaching of music. This can be seen in *Music from 5 to 16*[19] and the National Criteria for Music in the GCSE.[20] However, these moves towards 'eclecticism' are, in fact, a reflection of a view of education which is concerned with the development of different forms of understanding. In this context the justification for music is in terms of a way of knowing that combines cognitive and affective operations in a unique way. Music education is a process involving the initiation of pupils into the discipline. This is to be achieved through the inter-related experiential modes of performing, composing and listening, and the acquisition of appropriate skills and information. A well-known exponent of this position is Keith Swanwick. His book *A Basis for Music Education*[21] is often cited as providing one of the most comprehensive and acceptable rationales for music education in schools.

Differences of opinion in music education often appear to revolve round curriculum activities, the choice of materials and methods of teaching. But, as I have indicated, there are frequently other underlying disagreements. Any conception of music education will be dependent on ideas as to how music is justified as part of a programme of general education. Justifications for music are often seen as a 'political necessity', but what is more significant about a particular justification is that it relates to a wider view of education; this leads to a certain form of curriculum practice. Any general view of education will have a bearing on how one sees education in a specific curriculum area. For example, if education is to be understood as a preparation for adult life, then musical studies, if they are to count as *education*, will necessarily reflect the general principle in some way. Consequently, programmes would be concerned, ideally, with the acquisition of skills and techniques designed to enable pupils to participate in what are regarded as leisure pursuits: choirs, orchestras, ensembles, pop groups, brass bands and other corporate activities. At the very least the intention would be to provide experiences geared towards helping children become better 'consumers' of music. Of course, people who regard education as preparation for life might argue that music provides pupils with periods of relaxation which help them to pursue other more important work-related activities with renewed vigour and enthusiasm. If this were the case then the study of music would simply be an *aid* to education rather than music education itself. More progressive views of education sometimes lead to a type of practice that emphasizes 'exploration of sound', this being part of the process of self-realization and self-fulfilment. Notions of tradition and cultural background are rejected and replaced by 'immediacy', 'relevance' and 'interests'.

There is often much reference these days to the importance of pupils' enjoyment of music. It would be hard to disagree with the notion of enjoyment as a general educational aim applicable to all curriculum activities, for to enjoy something is to take satisfaction and delight in it for its own sake and not for some further end. However, enjoyment can also be a very misleading word. It is sometimes associated with pursuits which are simply pleasurable and not to be taken too seriously. But proper musical engagement — that which makes it meaningful — demands a sense of purpose and a great deal of application; it has to be worked at in an ordered and committed manner. This is not to imply that music is only for those who have been fully initiated into its mysteries through hours of toil and drudgery. However, it has to be acknowledged that unless children experience music as a serious and systematic form of study its meaningfulness is likely to be lost; any understanding of the discipline will be, at best, superficial.

I have already referred to the concept of liberal education. By this I mean a form of education available to all children and directed not towards some extrinsic end or specialist expertise. Rather it is concerned with the development of the individual's spiritual, moral, intellectual and aesthetic awareness through an understanding of the various types of human experience and knowledge. A commitment to the ideals of a liberal education leads to the view of music education as an 'immersion' into the discipline with emphasis on the fostering of musical 'joy' and 'understanding'. It is an approach to music education which aims to get children on the 'inside' of the discipline. In this way they come to understand and value its skills, techniques and procedures. Such an approach is essentially inclusive, emphasizing depth and breadth of knowledge and experience and the significance of both tradition and innovation in music. It is in the spirit of what Peter Abbs has called a 'conservationist' view of arts education;[22] it may be seen as a reaction against certain exclusive positions that have sometimes led to a narrow conception of music education and a denial of valuable forms of musical experience. In practice its methods are eclectic. They include a wide range of activities and a broad view of curriculum content; programmes are organized in a way that enables pupils to achieve a sense of competence and autonomy. I am not suggesting that this is an entirely new view of music education. A number of writers subscribe to such a position and many teachers are committed to forms of practice which embody these ideals.

However, it is an approach to music education which is in jeopardy if the arts are not given proper recognition in the National Curriculum. Although music now has a statutory place in the new order there remains a feeling of uncertainty and unease amongst those members of the teaching profession concerned with arts subjects. Few people would disagree with the principle that all children should have access to certain types of knowledge; yet the position and value of the arts within a broad and balanced education has never been clearly stated. Now that music has become optional at Key Stage 4 it may well again be regarded as a second-class subject. And with so much attention being given to the core components some teachers are of the opinion that music and the arts are being pushed ever more towards the periphery of the school curriculum. The purpose of this book is to argue for the significance of music in education as one of the six arts and, at the same time, to consider some of the practical implications of a conservationist aesthetic.

Notes and References

1 Ross, M. (1975) *Arts and the Adolescent*, Schools Council Working Paper No. 54, London, Evans.

2 Paynter, J. (1989) 'The Challenge of Creativity', *British Journal of Music Education*, 6, 2, pp. 235–237.

3 Swanwick, K. (1988) *Music, Mind and Education*, London, Routledge, p. 6.

4   SCHWAB, J. (1969) 'The Practical: A Language for Curriculum', *School Review*, 78, 1, pp. 1–23.
5   RAINBOW, B. (1968) 'The Historical and Philosophical Background to School Music Teaching', in RAINBOW, B. (Ed.) *Music Teachers Handbook*, London, Novello, pp. 21–32.
6   METCALFE, M. (1987) 'Towards the Condition of Music', in ABBS, P. (Ed.) *Living Powers: The Arts in Education*, London, Falmer Press, pp. 97–118.
7   BRACE, G. (1970) *Music and the Secondary School Timetable*, University of Exeter.
8   SCHOLES, P. (1947) *The Mirror of Music*, London, Novello.
9   INCORPORATED SOCIETY OF MUSICIANS (1947) *An Outline of Musical Education*, London, Curwen.
10 CENTRAL ADVISORY COUNCIL FOR EDUCATION (1963) *Half Our Future*, London, HMSO.
11 BEN-TOVIM, A. (1979) *Children and Music*, London, Black.
12 HOGGART, R. (1973) *Speaking to Each Other*, Vol. 1, Harmondsworth, Penguin, p. 81.
13 ROSS, M., *op. cit.*
14 WITKIN, R. (1974) *The Intelligence of Feeling*, London, Heinemann.
15 REID, L.A. (1986) *Ways of Understanding and Education*, London, Heinemann.
16 BEST, D. (1989) 'Feeling and Reason in the Arts: The Rationality of Feeling', in ABBS, P. (Ed.) *The Symbolic Order*, London, Falmer Press, pp. 70–85.
17 See, for example, PETERS, R.S. (1966) *Ethics and Education*, London, Gloucester, Allen and Unwin.
18 HINDEMITH, P. (1952) *A Composer's World*, Mass., Harvard University Press.
19 DES (1985) *Music from 5 to 16*, Curriculum Matters 4, London, HMSO.
20 DES (1985) *General Certificate of Secondary Education: The National Criteria: Music*, London, HMSO.
21 SWANWICK, K. (1979) *A Basis for Music Education*, Slough, NFER.
22 ABBS, P. (1987) *op. cit.*

Chapter 2

Musical Experience and Understanding

Introduction

Musical studies and experiences, within the context of a liberal
education, are concerned with the development of musical
understanding. Consequently, a central question for teachers
and all who are concerned with curriculum planning is, 'how
can this form of understanding be characterized and in what
ways can it be promoted through curriculum activities?'

Many musicians are often sceptical about 'theory', or
theorizing, especially when it gets in the way of practice.
Doubtless there are those who would argue that talking or
writing about music is largely a waste of time and nothing more
than an academic indulgence. Whilst I do not share this view it
is certainly worth remembering that any sort of theory or explanation is going to be both limited and provisional. The world
of music always seems to retain an indefinable magic and mystery which is beyond explanation. Indeed, these are the very
aesthetic qualities which capture our interest and imagination
and make music a constant source of delight.

But there are things which can be said (and need to be said)
about music and musical activity that will have implications,
although not necessarily directly, for the position of music in the
curriculum and also for curriculum design and implementation.
I shall not attempt to outline anything like a theory of musical
understanding, but I do want to further consider and develop
the principle of music as a way of knowing and understanding,

and put together a number of ideas which can eventually be related in educational practice. This will involve drawing on philosophical and psychological areas of inquiry, although the issues discussed in the separate sections are closely connected. Many readers will probably recognize some fairly well-trodden paths. I make no apology for this since there are several central themes and issues which are sufficiently important, and controversial, to warrant consideration in any debate on music education.

Music as Knowledge

In discussions on the theory of knowledge a distinction is often made between knowledge 'that' and knowledge 'how'. The former term refers to those things which are specified as verifiable propositions, whilst the latter is used to describe practical action or 'know-how'. Accordingly, it would be recognized that participation in musical activity involves a great deal of knowing how; how to play the scale of C major, how to hold the bow correctly, how to get the embouchure right. These are simple examples, and the development of musical techniques quite clearly involves the mastering of complex practical skills. There are also plenty of things to say and know 'about' music; we know 'that' Bach composed 48 Preludes and Fugues, 'that' a rag(a) is a mode in Indian music; 'that' the Kakaki is a tin trumpet played by the Hausa people of northern Nigeria. Such statements of fact can be shown to be true. On this view of knowledge, a statement like 'I know that my Redeemer liveth' would simply be a 'belief' rather than knowledge, since it would be impossible to 'prove' such an assertion in any empirical or logical way. Similarly, to say 'I know Beethoven's First Symphony', and implying something more than knowing 'about' it would, strictly speaking, be a misuse of the verb 'to know'.

Epistemological traditions which rest on the principle of knowledge as only that which can be stated in propositions have, of course, had an enormous influence on the ways in which people have come to view the world. They have also had a bearing on what has come to be regarded as significant and valuable, and indeed essential, in an educational context. For if education is taken to be concerned primarily with the development of 'rational' thinking through the acquisition and understanding of knowledge, and if knowledge is essentially a network of (true) propositions, then it is not hard to see why the arts have so frequently been regarded as of only peripheral concern. They might be useful for any number of reasons but they would not, and could not, be valued in terms of knowledge. Therefore, they would not be central to the educational process.

However, there are other less restricted ways of looking at knowledge and understanding, and more generous and optimistic attitudes towards education. Theories of knowledge inevitably contain, and rest on, certain sub-theories and in particular those of meaning and language. In attempting to characterize music as a way of knowing, a useful starting point is an examination of the idea that it might be regarded as a type of language or even a number of languages. This view is one that has attracted strong supporters and equally fervent opponents. It has often appealed to music educators. In their writings on the principles of teaching, eminent pedagogues such as Galin, Curwen and Yorke Trotter[1] clearly saw it as their task to instruct children in the 'reading', 'writing' and 'speaking' of the musical language. Of course, these educators were concerned primarily with the development of pupils' aural skills, which they considered to be the basis of musicianship training. In terms of teaching and learning 'music as language' became a convenient metaphor.

Nevertheless, the notion of the arts as languages or communication systems, in a more literal sense, is one that has occupied the minds of musicians, philosophers and psychologists over a fairly long period of time. John Dewey, for example, regarded music and other art forms as languages through which human meanings could be shared and exchanged, thus enabling people to communicate with each other in a unique way. But the meaning in an art work, for Dewey, is very different from the meaning in a scientific proposition. In fact, he maintains that science 'states' meanings whereas art 'expresses' them. For the purpose of distinguishing between these two types of meaning he comments:

the work of art certainly does not have that meaning
which is had by flags when used to signal another ship.
But it does have that possessed by flags when they are
used to decorate the deck of a ship for a dance.[2]

These days the remark may seem slightly quaint; but it is not
difficult to appreciate the point Dewey is making. He sees his
aesthetic theory as having a general applicability across the arts;
on his view, a musical work does not exactly mean *something*
that corresponds to an external reality or set of particular ideas.
But it is *meaningful* in that it incorporates and 'expresses' a
transformed feeling state which can be comprehended by the
sympathetic listener. The arts are languages because they are
expressive forms (and indeed the highest forms) of human communication that enable people to 'say' things to each other
which cannot be 'said' in any other way. What is rather strange,
however, about Dewey's theory, from the point of view of
language, is that although he talks a geat deal about sharing and
communication he also places considerable emphasis on indi-
vidualized experience; this occurs when there is 'creative col-
laboration' between art product and respondent. Consequently,
a composition does not have one meaning but an infinite number. This, of course, is a popular view. But in a way it under-
mines the language theory since he seems to move away from
the significance of 'public' meaning. How can there be language
without public meaning?

For those who find Dewey's position vague and unconvinc-
ing (in terms of meaning and language) Derek Cooke's[3] analysis
of tonal music, and his subsequent theory of music as the
language of the emotions, may appear to represent a more
acceptable view of meaning. Cooke claims that it is possible to
identify a basic 'vocabulary' and 'laws' of musical language;
composers use these for the purpose of imparting fairly precise
public 'messages'. He gives many examples to illustrate how
certain intervals and intervalic patterns have been used consis-
tently to convey particular emotions such as joy, suffering and
grief. Within a work these basic meanings are always modified
through combination with the 'vitalizing' agents of rhythm,
timbre and volume. But however subtle, inventive or original

the composer may be, he or she is always governed by internal 'laws' of the language. In other words composers, and all musicians, have to operate within the confines of a publically accepted framework. The language or tradition is always greater than the individual.

Cooke has been criticized on the grounds of inconsistency and philosophical naivity, but, as he himself pointed out, his work is not philosophical. Essentially it is musicological. His very detailed and impressive analysis is a study of musical structures and how those structures determine the ways in which sounds can and cannot be used. And although he is concerned exclusively with tonal music there is no logical reason why his general thesis should not apply to other styles.[4] Certainly within the framework of classical tonality there are identifiable and familiar 'rules'. These are not simply the old and rather despised rules of harmony and counterpoint found in textbooks and theory manuals. Rather, they are a set of accepted conventions which somehow limit the use of 'material' and consequently define and validate structure. We might contemplate the music of the great masters and marvel at their ingenuity, their ability to 'break' the rules and stretch the musical framework to its limits; but it nevertheless remains to form what is sometimes described as 'background'. And it is against this background, gradually assimilated through the processes of enculturation and education, that we are able to make sense of individual musical items. Unfamiliar backgrounds, such as music from non-western cultures are often confusing. According to a Hans Keller,[5] *lack* of background in certain types of contemporary music actually renders them meaning*less*. What is difficult to accept about Cooke's referential theory is the direct connection made between meaning and emotion. Are composers really telling us something about their emotional states through their compositions? I think it is unlikely that Cooke ever intended to say anything quite as simple as this. However, we are left with the impression that the innermost secrets of the composer's heart are to be eventually discovered through the development of more highly refined analytical techniques.

The general opposition to the idea of music as a language as portrayed in different ways by Dewey and Cooke, arises from the view that music does not possess the necessary features of language. In her famous book *Philosophy in a new Key* Suzanne Langer[6] skilfully marshals arguments to support a theory of music as the 'logical expression' of human feeling. Music has meaning which is made manifest through 'expressive' and 'significant' form. However, she maintains that music cannot be a language because it does not possess the essential qualities and characteristics. These include, most notably, 'dictionary definitions' and syntactical rules. It is for this reason that she prefers to say that music has 'import' (rather than meaning), this being an articulation of emotive experience which can be 'felt' but never defined in a 'conventionally fixed' manner. The notion of music as language is *logically* unacceptable. Similar objections to the language theory have been made by Hindemith.[7] He also argues that music has neither 'stable connotation' nor the 'usual properties' of language. This is taken further by Peter Scrimshaw[8] who refers to the more general features of language such as translatability and the principles of negation; quite clearly these do not apply to music. On these views, then, music cannot be a language other than in a metaphorical sense.

An interesting and very different position has been adopted by Paul Hirst.[9] He suggests that those who oppose the languages theory of art do so simply because of their insistence on the idea of naming and reference as being central to language. If it is possible to put aside what he considers to be a mistaken theory of meaning then one may be able to look at music and the arts in an entirely new way. Drawing on Wittgenstein, Hirst argues that meaning and understanding exist in the *use* of language and are built up in the public use of symbols. In other words, meaning exists in a particular context and does not depend on dictionary definitions or agreed referents. Accordingly, music (and other art forms) might be seen as an example of what Wittgenstein called the 'language game'. A similar Wittgensteinian approach is taken by David Aspin[10] who holds the view that what is central to language is shared contextual meanings. These are certainly not confined to the discursive mode; sounds, signs, gestures and movements can all become networks of significance.

How *far* meaning in discursive language can be reduced entirely to the use of symbols in context nevertheless remains contentious. It has been argued that all languages pre-suppose a world which is independent of our minds and determines the truth or fallacy of statements.[11] But the principle outlined by Hirst and Aspin does provide an intriguing way of looking at non-verbal pursuits. Ordinary games are interesting examples. In football, for instance, the actions of the players do have meaning for those who understand the rules and procedures of the game. A long forward pass is meaningful, within the context of the game, to both players and spectators insofar as they understand the workings of the game. To the outsider, who knows nothing of football, the action is no more than one of the players kicking the ball; as an outsider he or she cannot 'read' the game. This is not to liken music to football, or any other sport, but the notion of the *'language game'*, in which the meaning of sounds depends on their use in a context might be a very fruitful way of characterizing that 'form of life' which we call music. The plausibility of the position becomes particularly apparent in compositional or improvisatory activities; here we are very aware that the use of sounds does have to conform to the rules and conventions of a particular style or genre. It is with knowledge of these 'correct' uses that we make decisions and judgements as to what is 'right', 'wrong', 'effective', 'weak' and so forth, and it is when people can make and act on these judgements that they display a certain 'musical understanding'. These views might be compared with those of formalist writers who regard music as a 'self-enclosed' system; the meaning of music is in the music. Perhaps this is what Stravinsky was intimating when he said that 'the one true comment on a piece of music is another piece of music'.[12]

Although there are clearly many different ideas about the meanings in music, I personally find the language theory, and the notion of 'meaning is the use', to be very convincing since it conforms (at least to some extent) to my understanding of music as a practitioner. It points to music as being a rule-governed system or a form of discourse. Understanding requires a grasp of music's 'grammar' or more precisely 'grammars'. The grammars will not be learned exclusively through formal educational programmes but their existence does have important implications for curriculum design and practice.

For Paul Hirst the languages theory of art is the basis of a view of music as a type of knowledge. Although his propositional theory of art has been widely criticized by philosophers it has led to the opening up of a wider debate (which was probably Hirst's intention) about artistic knowing, and an increased interest in an alternative epistemological position; and this alternative epistemology is of the greatest importance not only to arts educators but to all concerned with educational planning and decision making.

In 1965 Hirst presented what was to become a highly influential paper entitled 'Liberal Education and the Nature of Knowledge'.[13] He argued that human beings have developed distinct ways or 'forms' of knowing: mathematics, natural sciences, history, fine arts, religion and philosophy. The forms should constitute the basis of a liberal education for all children. Education is essentially a matter of developing people's thinking capacities through the different ways in which we come to know and understand reality. Each 'form' is said to have central concepts, a logical structure, particular procedural methods and distinctive tests for truth. Hirst subsequently outlined the separate forms in greater detail. Using the language theory of art he hypothesized that musical statements (e.g. a symphony) might be thought of as propositions (knowing 'that') which have a parallel with propositions in science, mathematics and other forms. Accordingly, musical propositions would employ musical concepts in a rule-governed way and could ultimately be judged to be true or false. In talking about musical concepts Hirst does not mean things like pitch, rhythm, timbre and volume. He compares a pattern of notes or sounds with a concept in normal discourse. Such patterns become meaningful when combined with others in a particular context.

This propositional account has a certain logic but it also raises a number of awkward questions. To begin with what sense can be made of the idea that a musical work might be 'true' or 'false'? The argument is that notions of truth and falsity can only be understood in relation to a particular form of knowledge. In the arts, empirical evidence or logical status are inappropriate criteria for determining truth and falsity. 'Truth' depends on the possibility of those on the 'inside' of the arts, i.e. *the cognescenti*, being able to come to some objective agreement as to what counts as the 'correct' use of artistic concepts and statements.

This question of objective standards is, of course, a central issue in any theory of art; it is one that has significant consequences for arts education. There are those who would subscribe to a form of subjectivism and say that 'good' or 'bad' are simply expressions of individual reactions to art statements.[14] Others might claim that all artistic judgements are 'relative' and dependent on the particular *social* context in which such judgements are being made. In a trivial sense this is obviously the case, but there is a world of music in which we operate and where we can, and frequently do, make objective judgements about the 'correctness' or otherwise of, say, a melody or piece of harmony. And unless such judgements can be made there can be no meaning in music. The fact that we can talk about 'great' works of art, 'outstanding composers' and the like indicates a measure of agreement amongst musicians; it is this agreement which makes music a discourse and a meaningful form of activity. Certainly, these agreements change from time to time, and at any one time there will be disputes and disagreements; but this applies to every area of knowledge and understanding. However, I am not sure we ever go as far as to talk about a musical work as being false although we may agree that it is of little musical importance and merit.

What is totally lacking in the propositional account is any recognition of the fact that when people say they 'know' a piece of music there is an implication of some sort of 'feeling response' to the work. Certainly, as we have seen, there are differences of opinion regarding the connections between music and emotional or feeling states. But all aesthetic theories (even formalist theories) recognize the feeling dimension. We talk about the charm and beauty of music; we are moved and excited by performances. In performance we are constantly striving to bring out expressive elements, for without these elements music is devoid of meaning. For Louis Arnaud Reid to know an art work is to have a relationship with it, or to be acquainted with it, in a way which goes far beyond recognizing and evaluating its internal structure and coherence. This may be described as 'feeling for', 'love of', 'enjoyment of'; but whatever phrase is used it refers to what Reid calls 'aesthetic knowing'.[15] Reid maintains that we can only properly know art from 'within' — from 'direct experience'. Those who deny this 'acquaintance' to be knowledge have simply failed to grasp the full import of artistic experience. Using a musical example Reid reinforces this point in the following manner:

> To call it (artistic knowledge) enriched acquaintance only, denying it to be knowledge is only a verbal operation, a concession to a far too limited conception of knowledge, dominated by one form of it, the propositional. And the operation fails. For how does the 'enrichment' of aesthetic apprehension of the parts of a fugue, in relation to one another and the whole, grow from vagueness into clarity of understanding, if there is no growth of knowledge of the fugue (which is certainly not identical with the things I can say about it). Is this not an increase in knowledge, if I do not know the fugue better, and so have more knowledge of it (and not merely about it) what is it? Is not the experience of emergent, aesthetic meaning an increase of knowledge?[16]

I think this is one of the clearest and most concise descriptions of aesthetic knowing. It not only exposes the limitation of the propositional theory but also captures the very essence of meaningful musical engagement. Reid's position is, of course, very much in line with that of Suzanne Langer whose seminal writings on the arts are in fundamental opposition to the propositional theories of the positivist tradition. Inspired and influenced by a number of different philosophical schools of thought she also developed a theory which extends the notion of knowledge to 'ordered experiences'. Focusing on the symbolic nature of art, myth and ritual she outlined a conception of the arts which constituted a major challenge to the prevailing epistemology. For Langer the arts are symbolic modes of thinking and understanding. They express the human condition in a unique manner, and are just as meaningful, in their own ways, as anything which can be stated in logically or empirically verifiable propositions. For those who insist on the primacy of the propositional (or even an 'extended' view of propositions) then direct experience of music and the arts cannot, on its own be regarded as a way of knowing. But anybody on the 'inside' of the arts will recognize the limitation of this position and appreciate the full power and significance of aesthetic knowing.

Although Reid (like Langer) would not regard music as a language I see no reason why the language theory (based on the principle of *meaning is the use*) should necessarily be incompatible with aesthetic knowing. An important part of understanding music is to be aware of structural patterns and systems of organization. As I said earlier, music which is set against an unfamiliar structure or background often becomes difficult to comprehend. It is for this reason that people are 'turned off' some types of contemporary or non-western idioms. On the other hand there is certainly more to musical understanding than simply being aware of its structural design; but we can only fully appreciate this when we are engaged in musical activity. This is one of the main problems of talking about music and music education.

Intelligent engagement in music involves the continuous merging of the cognitive and the affective in a particular type of thinking, namely, *musical* thinking. Because of the influence of the propositional view of knowing, with its emphasis on 'words', it is only fairly recently that we have come to talk of musical *thinking*. However, there is a growing recognition of a variety of thinking styles; more recent psychological research into the nature of intelligence is providing a major challenge to many established assumptions about the range and styles of human abilities.

Musical Intelligence

In the Introduction to *Living Powers*, Peter Abbs[17] refers to a remarkable self-portait painted by a 14 year-old boy. As a result of performance on a standard I.Q. test, this pupil was considered to be of below-average intelligence. Many teachers of music could probably cite parallel examples of children who display particular musical talent but are otherwise regarded as low achievers. That such pupils are categorized in this pessimistic way is indicative of an attitude that has been prevalent in education for many years. The arts are seen as extras. Although it is 'nice' for pupils to be engaged in artistic pursuits, their achievements, or lack of them, are of little concern. Educational progress is measured largely in terms of 'success' in Language, Mathematics and the Natural Sciences — the very (propositional) subjects that now form the 'core' of the National Curriculum.

These areas of knowledge are obviously directly related to a view of human intelligence in which linguistic, logico-mathematical and spatial thinking are regarded as the central cognitive operations. Although this is so obviously a very partial and restricted view of human intelligence it is one which nevertheless permeates educational thinking. But if a pupil is an excellent instrumentalist and can participate effectively in an orchestra or ensemble is he not also exhibiting intelligent behaviour? For to be intelligent means to act in intelligent ways in particular circumstances. To talk about an individual being intelligent, or showing intelligence, means little without reference to a symbolic area of activity and understanding. Why should this be limited to linguistic and mathematical related modes? There is musically intelligent behaviour dependent on a distinctive type of thinking which is essentially musical. In spite of what is commonly assumed to be the case, thinking is not confined to verbal operations. To compose, arrange, perform or apprehend is to think in the 'language' of music.

And yet it has been widely accepted that musical competence and ability is something separate from 'general intelligence'. This has often been taken for granted by those researchers who have investigated and attempted to measure musical ability or aptitude. In his famous treatise on the psychology of music Carl Seashore[18] concludes that effective musical behaviour consists of a combination of 'musical talent' and 'intelligence'. Following Seashore, Arnold Bentley[19] found little positive correlation between musical ability and intelligence as measured by standardized tests. Both of these reseachers, working in the psychometric tradition, have had a marked influence on music education practice and especially on the ways in which individual pupils have been selected for instrumental tuition. But they have also reinforced the idea of musical ability as being something different from intelligence, and there have been numerous psychological studies based on this assumption which have been summarized by Shuter-Dyson and Gabriel[20] in their extensive review of the subject. Consequently, there exists the commonly held and rather curious (if not absurd) view of one person who might be seen as musical but not very intelligent as opposed to another who might be regarded as intelligent but not very musical. As a result of more recent research in the fields of cognitive and developmental psychology these older ideas are being replaced by alternative conceptions of intelligence. There are new views of musical thinking and understanding.

In a book entitled *Frames of Mind*[21] Professor Howard Gardner of Harvard University has outlined what he calls a theory of 'multiple intelligences'. His findings are of the greatest interest to musicians and music educators. I believe Gardner's work is a major contribution to the development of a completely different awareness of the significance of the arts in society and in education. He argues that the classical view of intelligence is narrow and limited to only certain types of cognitive operations. But there is, he claims, persuasive evidence for the existence of several relatively autonomous human competencies, or frames of mind, which can be fashioned and combined in many ways by individuals and cultures. Gardner draws on different fields of inquiry to support his thesis — biological sciences, medicine, psychology, philosophy, education — and suggests six types of intelligence: linguistic, logical-mathematical, musical, spatial, bodily-kinesthetic and personal. The evidence for an intelligence depends on the identification of 'pre-requisites' such as a set of problem-solving skills and the potential for 'creating problems' leading to the development of new knowledge. There are also 'signs' or 'criteria'; these include the existence of specific intellectual skills, exceptional individuals, a set of core operations, a distinct developmental and evolutionary history, support from experimental and psychometric findings and the susceptibility to encoding in a symbol system. In a very impressive and cogent manner Gardner shows how music meets these criteria. He goes on to suggest that musical competence is relatively undeveloped in members of Western Societies because, on the whole, it is not valued. But since music is one of the main forms of human intelligence it should, in Gardner's opinion, be central to education.

Gardner is, of course, by no means alone in holding this wider view of intelligence. Another theory which supports the concept of a separate musical intelligence is the 'structure of intellect' model of intelligence developed and refined by Professor J.P. Guilford.[22] For Guilford, intelligence is not one set of operations; it is a multi-dimensional *process* with many different components. His model suggests that there are numerous ways in which people can be intelligent. Musical operations are a form of thinking which can be recognized as distinct from those other types of cognitive functions that are often considered to be the main indicators of intelligence. Guilford has shown much interest in creativity as an aspect of intelligence and I shall refer to his work again in Chapter 6. During the last decade or so there have been major advances in research into the different aspects of musical thinking. These post-Piagetian developments owe much to Howard Gardner and others working in the field of cognitive psychology. Two important contributors, in this country, are David Hargreaves[23] and John Sloboda[24] who are musicians as well as psychologists. Both have drawn together and developed a wide variety of findings, and provided detailed accounts of musical operations within a coherent theoretical framework.

What is significant about all of these psychological theories and research findings is that they establish a new way of considering musical thinking as a distinct type of intelligence. This is in sharp contrast to long-held assumptions which currently underpin educational policies in this and many other countries. In the opening chapter I mentioned Cardinal Newman's view of music as being an 'elegant pastime'. The basis of his opposition to music as an educational activity was that 'it does not form or cultivate the intellect'.[25] In many ways these ideas are just as common as they were a hundred years ago and they continue to influence all aspects of educational planning and practice. It could be fairly argued that our educational system is founded on an outdated conception of knowledge and intelligence; it is therefore hardly surprising that music and the other arts continue to be regarded as marginal concerns. But as Gardner has so rightly pointed out:

> For most of humanity, and throughout most of human history, the processes and products involved in artistic creation have been far more pervasive than those employed in the sciences. In fact, logical scientific thought can be considered an invention of the West in the wake of the Renaissance — an invention which is still restricted to a small enclave of thinkers; participation in the literary, musical or graphical arts, on the other hand, has been widespread for thousands of years.[26]

Conclusions

My comments on music as a way of knowing and understanding constitute only the briefest sketch of what is an extremely complex area of inquiry. Many of the issues raised have been treated in much more detail elsewhere.[27]

What does emerge from more recent work in the fields of epistemology and cognitive psychology is that, through their unique ability to create symbolic systems, humans have developed different rule-governed categories of discourse. The truly remarkable achievement and sophistication of discursive language is unquestionable; but changing views of knowledge and intelligence have led to a re-awakening of the recognition that the transmission of meanings is not confined to the linguistic mode. Unfortunately, the arts have often been regarded as mere expressions of pent-up emotions or simply pleasurable sensations, but the sounds, signs, marks and movements which constitute the discourse of the arts are themselves symbolic systems with their own styles of rationality, their own structures and their own procedural principles. People engage in musical pursuits *intelligently* and according to the canons of the discipline.

All societies have their aesthetic systems because artistic discourse is basic to the human condition. This is emphasized in the writings of Dewey and Langer and given psychological re-inforcement by Gardner. A similar view is outlined by Sloboda[28] who refers to the work of Chomsky and Schenker to illustrate connections between linguistic and musical operations. Through the process of evolution men and women have acquired a capacity (or cognitive apparatus) for the development of language and other symbolic modes or intelligences. These intelligences are shaped and transmitted through a particular culture, but they will only thrive and develop if recognized and valued; they have to be stimulated and nurtured in an appropriate environment.

There is, then, a new awareness of the significance of music and the arts. This relates directly to the question of their place in a system of education designed to introduce pupils to the full range of human meanings. It there is a sincere desire to provide a broad and balanced education for our children then the arts can no longer be viewed as 'luxuries' which are available only if time permits. They must be accepted as important areas of understanding which need to be treated as seriously as other branches of knowledge.

From the point of view of the music curriculum the most obvious conclusion is that pupils will need to follow balanced and well-designed programmes. Children require opportunities to get on the inside of the discipline in order to appreciate and grasp its 'workings'. Disjointed and casual experience will not achieve this end; pupils will have to master necessary skills, techniques, procedures and methods (i.e. the 'grammars' of music) to understand what it is to be involved in musical pursuits, and come to know (in the broadest sense) 'how music goes'.

Systematic planning is clearly a necessary requirement. We readily accept the need for this in some curriculum areas, but in the arts programmes have often been haphazard and fragmentary. According to recent reports this is still the case in some schools.[29] If we genuinely want to promote musical intelligence then proper provision for ordered and structured schemes of teaching and learning is a major priority. However, in saying this I do not have in mind some national scheme which would prescribe the curriculum in all schools as being the only way forward.

Educational practice in school operates against the background of a wide number of theoretical constructs. Teaching is never a matter of simply settling for the most attractive theory and using this as a basis for working out pedagogical strategies. It is more a process of constantly questioning, modifying, elaborating and reflecting on one's own theoretical perspectives for the purpose of devising teaching approaches which have an adequate justification and are likely to be effective in practice. The value of considering the different theoretical positions referred to in the preceding sections is that they provide reference points and 'feed in' to what is an on-going and highly complex practical enterprise. In the following two chapters I shall critically examine some principles of curriculum design and curriculum implementation in the light of the views of musical experience and understanding so far considered.

Notes and References

1 See SIMPSON, K. (1975) *Some Great Music Educators*, London, Novello.

2 DEWEY, J. (1958) *Art as Experience*, New York, Capricorn Books, p. 83 (first puplished 1934).

3 COOKE, D. (1959) *The Language of Music*, Oxford, Oxford University Press.

4 See REID, L.A. (1969) *Meaning in the Arts*, London, Allen and Unwin, pp. 133–138.

5 KELLER, H. (1966) 'Wolfgang Amadeus Mozart', in SIMPSON, R. (Ed.) *The Symphony*, Vol. 1, Harmondsworth, Pelican.

6 LANGER, S. (1957) *Philosophy in a New Key*, 3rd ed., Boston, Harvard University Press.

7 HINDEMITH, P. (1952) *A Composer's World*, Gloucester, Mass Harvard University Press, p. 41.

8   SCRIMSHAW, P. (1973) 'Statements, language and art: some comments on Professor Hirst's paper', *Cambridge Journal of Education*, *3*, 3, p. 44.

9   HIRST, P. (1974) *Knowledge and the Curriculum*, London, Routledge.

10 ASPIN, D. (1984) *Objectivity and Assessment in the Arts The Problem of Aesthetic Education*, London, National Association for Education in the Arts.

11 See PRING, R.A. (1976) *Knowledge and Schooling*, London Open Books, p. 44.

12 STRAVINSKY, I. and CRAFT, R. (1961) *Dialogues and a Diary*, London, Faber, pp. 62–63.

13 HIRST, P. (1974) *op. cit.*, pp. 30–53.

14 An interesting discussion of this issue is to be found in WHITE, J.P. (1968) 'Creativity and Education: a philosophical analysis', *British Journal of Educational Studies*, *16*, 2, pp. 123–127.
    See also, HAMLYN, D. (1972) 'Objectivity', in DEARDEN, R.F., HIRST, P.H. and PETERS, R.S. (Eds) *Education and the Development of Reason*, London, Routledge.

15 REID, L.A. (1986) *Ways of Understanding and Education*, London, Heinemann, p. 42.

16 REID, L.A. (1969) *op. cit.*, p. 211.

17 ABBS, P. (1987) *Living Powers: The Arts in Education*, London, Falmer Press, p. 1.

18 SEASHORE, C. (1967) *Psychology of Music*, New York, Dover Publications (first published 1938).

19 BENTLEY, A. (1966) *Musical Ability in Children and its Measurement*, London, Harrap.

20 SHUTER-DYSON, R. and GABRIEL, C. (1981) *The Psychology of Musical Ability*, 2nd ed., London, Methuen.

21 GARDNER, H. (1984) *Frames of Mind: The Theory of Multiple Intelligences*, London, Heinemann.

22 GUILFORD, J.P. (1975) 'Creativity: A Quarter Century of Progress', in TAYLOR, I. and GETZELS, J. (Eds) *Perspectives in Creativity*, Chicago, Aldine.

23 HARGREAVES, D. (1986) *The Developmental Psychology of Music*, Cambridge, Cambridge University Press.

24 SLOBODA, J. (1985) *The Musical Mind*, Oxford, Clarendon Press.

25 NEWMAN, J.H. (1852) *The Idea of a University*, Discourse VI, (Ed. MARTIN, J.) London, Reinhart Press, p. 109.
26 GARDNER, H. (1982) 'Artistry following Damage to the Human Brain' in ELLIS, A. (Ed.) *Normality and Pathology in Cognitive Functions*, London, Academic Press, p. 299.
27 See, for example SCRUTON, R. (1983) *The Aesthetic Understanding*, London, Methuen. See also GARDNER (1984) *op. cit.*
28 SLOBODA, J. (1985) *op. cit.*, Chapter 1.
29 For example, DES (1989) *Standards in Education, 1988–89. The Annual Report of HM Senior Chief Inspector of Schools*, London, HMSO.

Chapter 3

The Music Curriculum

Introduction

Most children receive musical instruction in class lessons at some stage of compulsory schooling; following the Education Reform Act this should eventually become an entitlement for all pupils between the ages of 5 and 14 (music is now optional at Key Stage 4). In many schools there are also various musical activities beyond the classroom. I suggested in the opening chapter that the extracurricular pursuits which have become an accepted, and increasingly *expected*, part of the musical and social life of educational institutions, should also be regarded as part of the music education enterprise. However, I shall leave discussion of school choirs, orchestras, ensemble groups and other 'voluntary' activities until Chapter 6.

I want to concentrate, for the present, on music as a time-tabled subject and focus on the content and design of curricula. It is, of course, impossible to talk of content in isolation. In practice, the curriculum is not simply a body of knowledge or subject matter; it is a dynamic *process*. The curriculum is 'alive' and consists in the actions and interactions of teachers and pupils. Models, frameworks and programmes of study are not curricula in themselves, although they can form the *basis* for curriculum strategies. This is something which is often forgotten in the current educational climate. In spite of all the documentation curriculum *issues* are actually becoming over-simplified. In fact, they are far from being simple or straightforward.

Discussions of content inevitably lead to a consideration of teaching and learning processes, but I shall examine teaching more closely in the following chapter. My intention, here, is not to *prescribe* a particular content. Rather it is to highlight some of the critical issues that arise in connection with decisions about curriculum planning and the selection of content.

Musical Activities

A frequent criticism of much class music teaching in recent years, particularly at secondary level, has been the amount of time devoted to the acquisition of information or knowledge 'about' music. One reason for the growth of 'musicological' study is that it gives music a certain 'academic respectability'. And because of the old divisive separation between academic and practical subjects in some schools it is not hard to see how this situation has arisen. It would, of course, be strange if children did not come to know something about the composers whose works they performed and listened to, instruments they might play, or the social and historical aspects of music as an art form. This type of background knowledge is not insignificant and will be especially important in critical studies of music. But obviously tasks like writing notes about composers, drawing instruments or copying out time charts, are, *on their own*, poor substitutes for those practical activities which afford opportunities for direct musical engagement and experience. Pupils are not keen on learning too much 'about' music:

> At the moment we're doing those history charts. I find those boring because all we're doing is writing out about those different composers and what year they were in or whatever, but sometimes we sing in class, and that's good.[1]

I am sure that such an attitude is by no means atypical. Pupils want to *do* things in their music lessons, and it is through practical activities that they develop musical understanding. It is probable (although by no means certain) that the majority of music teachers now support the principle of 'direct contact' with music as a basis for curriculum practice. Nevertheless, there are alternative interpretations of this principle. 'Traditional' performance activities or 'progressive' explorations of sound materials are both forms of direct musical experience, but they are likely to have little similarity in content and style and may well be defended for different reasons.

During the past few years there has emerged what might be called a new orthodoxy, namely, that all children should experience music through performing, composing and listening activities. The origins of this idea can probably be traced back to Rousseau or even Aristotle, and it is a view that has been successively endorsed by distinguished music educators such as Percy Scholes, Walford Davies, Kenneth Simpson and Keith Swanwick. From the 1970s the performing-composing-listening model has provided the framework for numerous documents published by the Department of Education and Science and many Local Education Authorities. *And it is a very good model.* If children are to have a broad and comprehensive musical education aimed towards developing their musical intelligence they clearly need to be introduced to the essential methods of the discipline. Singing a few songs or listening to the occasional record is hardly the way to initiate children into the world of music. Although many educators agree that the three experiential modes should consititute the core of music programmes there are those who express reservations about accepting the model too readily. For example, is it necessary for pupils to be involved in *all* three modes in order to attain musical understanding? Is one of more consequence than the others? Are they of equal importance? These questions need to be addressed since there are alternative views which suggest a variety of approaches to curriculum planning.

In what was for some time a very influential book dealing with the content of the curriculum, John White[2] argues strongly against the hypothesis that in order to 'appreciate' art it is necessary to participate in 'creating' it for oneself. He links this argument to 'performance' and refers quite explicitly to music. White maintains that there is no 'empirical evidence' to support the idea that performing and creating are necessary pre-requisites for developing a 'love' of art. Since he sees this as the purpose of arts education, a music programme should be one that concentrates essentially on 'appreciation'; the intention would be to develop in pupils a discriminating sense of taste and value. Here then is a view from an eminent educational philosopher and curriculum theorist which is in sharp contrast to what many music educators have been advocating in recent years. Does it have any credibility or is it simply the misconceived 'theory' of an 'outsider'?

Although White considers knowledge of the arts to be an important part of a liberal education, he appears to hold a somewhat restricted (although not uncommon) view of the scope of artistic experience. His idea of music education would seem to be a process concerned with the development of 'musical criticism' or 'connoisseurship'. The emergent picture of the musically educated person is the conventional listener or 'consumer'; somebody who would appreciate a 'good' performance of a Brahms symphony at the Festival Hall. Whether or not people who take part in music making are 'better' or more sophisticated consumers is perhaps a question which could be best answered empirically. But it is likely that active participants would respond to performances of musical works in a *particular* way; and it is difficult to imagine anybody on the inside of the performing arts not subscribing to this view. White's outlook represents a typical example of what I would call an old-fashioned 'appreciationist' conception of music education; to many music teachers it would seem reactionary and dated. However, I am inclined to think that there are quite a few people, not directly involved in music education but nevertheless in positions of some influence, who still think of musical studies in this limited way. It would, of course, be quite wrong to say that without the experience of performing and composing *no* musical understanding can be achieved; that is manifestly not so. But the point is that to know and understand the discipline of music is not merely to recognize and value musical forms. Essentially, it is to be acquainted with a 'form of life'. This includes responding to compositions and making evaluative judgements about them, and also involves creating and performing music, since these are the distinct and interrelated methods of the discipline. Any proper music *education* will be concerned with activities which promote an understanding of these methods. This may seem obvious enough to the musician; but artistic 'contemplation' and 'consumption' have had a singularly powerful influence on the way many people have come to regard the study of music in an educational context. The model for music education has often been the 'concert-goer' rather than the musician. Ideally, musical studies will include both participatory and evaluative activities; and, of course, the former always incorporates the latter.

If children are to become 'musicians' they will be required to learn something of the 'workings' of music through action. This involves assimilating and coming to understand the basic *procedural* principles of the discipline. In a typical choral activity, for example, there are many different procedures to be followed: — watching, listening to instructions, being ready to start, holding music correctly; attending to pulse, rhythms, pitch, dynamics; taking account of the style of the music being performed; attending to the 'rise' and 'fall' of phrases, controlling a crescendo or diminuendo, being aware of the music's expressive character. These are but a few of the procedures which apply to music making at all levels, and to follow them is what it is to be engaged in a musical activity. It is through the procedures that we get a 'feel' for music and a knowledge of how the discipline 'works'. The procedures have to be *learned*; people are not automatically aware of them.

Again, these comments might seem obvious and perhaps even trivial. But one of the reasons why children (and many adults) never really get going on musical activities is because they have not internalized these procedures. This is not to imply that performance has to be highly regimented or controlled in an authoritarian fashion; far from it. But unless musical activity is conducted in accordance with the appropriate methods — unless it is done properly — it loses its point and meaning; and the same principle will apply to any activity which is not pursued in a rule-governed and ordered way. It also needs to be realized that the learning of musical procedures is not easy. The process is rigorous and demanding, requiring much guidance, correction, intervention, encouragement and critical response on the part of a *teacher*.

The procedural principles referred to above would be particularly applicable to those activities such as class singing or class orchestra. However, these represent only one type of performance experience. Singing in a choir, playing in an orchestra or taking part in some sort of class performance does not constitute quite the same type of experience as participating as a member of a string quartet or a pop group, or performing as a soloist. In the case of a choir (or class singing lesson) it is the conductor (or teacher) who has the job of ensuring that the procedures are being followed by those taking part. Members of small ensemble groups and individual performers require a degree of musical *independence*. This independence is vitally important in the development of musical understanding, just as it is in any other area of disciplined activity. A legitimate criticism of programmes which are entirely class performance-based is that children rarely have the opportunity of making independent decisions. It is perhaps for this reason that some educators have attached so much significance to group composition (or creative music making) since this type of activity necessarily involves pupils working in an independent manner. But it is also quite possible for children to participate in small-group performance which offers opportunities for them to make their own musical decisions. There are plenty of published materials specifically designed for this purpose.

Compositional activity, of one sort or another, has become an accepted feature of class music teaching. It is sometimes maintained that children can and should experience music as composers. This claim needs to be looked at carefully. Children might be said to be involved in a process something like that of the composer since they are 'selecting', 'rejecting' and 'relating' musical materials and attempting to fashion them into some finished product. However, investigations into creative processes, although limited, indicate that there are considerable *differences* in the ways that composers approach their work.[3] There is no standard compositional method. Therefore if children are said to be working as composers it would need to be stated which particular composer was being taken as the model.

To model a composition on somebody else's music is common practice; to model a composition on somebody's *processes* seems rather peculiar.

It is very important to clarify these issues. So much of the criticism of creative or compositional activity has been based on the truism that children in school do not have the knowledge and techniques of established composers. But compositional activities are of the greatest value in that they enable pupils to develop an insight into the techniques and structures of music, or what in the last chapter I called the 'grammar' and 'language' of music. These activities offer further opportunities for children to develop musical understanding; the principles of procedure are experienced directly and with a growing independence. In the light of my own experience as a class teacher I would also want to add that most pupils seem to be highly motivated by compositional activities. They enjoy taking part and show great interest in listening to each other's musical 'ideas'.

Traditionally, musicians have studied melody writing, harmony and counterpoint. Sometimes this type of work has been very formal, some would say restrictive, and dominated by the 'rules' of Macpherson, Kitson, Lovelock, *et al.* Many musicians, particularly performers, sometimes wonder why they have to learn these techniques; the study of harmony and counterpoint is often regarded as a tedious chore. The value of 'paperwork' studies (if well taught) is that through them people come to a greater understanding of music as a symbolic system. And, of course, there is no reason why practice in formal harmony and counterpoint should be uninteresting, unimaginative or uncreative. Now I am not suggesting that all pupils in school should study formal harmony in the way that specialist music students might still do so, but the experience of producing one's own music is an important part of musicianship training. The unfortunate thing about compositional activity in the classroom is that it has sometimes led to a *laissez-faire* type of practice. Some people seem to have held the view that whatever children do is valuable; for teachers to 'intefere' is to stifle pupils' creativity. William Murphy, for example, writing about creative music in the primary school, talks about the importance of the teacher restricting his role to 'organizing'. He warns of the 'dangers' of 'suggesting ideas which could possibly have a narrowing effect'.[4] Whatever was *meant* by this sort of advice it has often resulted in non-musical experimentation; this has discredited a pedagogical movement which has otherwise offered new and exciting forms of musical experience. Clearly children cannot 'create' or 'compose' out of nothing. They need plenty of background ideas and suggestions; the teacher has a *central* role providing pupils with guidance and direction.

Musical Skills

Effective participation in performing and composing activities is partly dependent on children having acquired certain musical skills. There is a growing opinion that the importance of skill acquisition has often been overlooked in both curriculum planning and practice. Indeed, there were times when to mention the word 'skill' was to risk being accused of adopting an anti-educational stance. But music is a highly skilful discipline; this needs to be taken into account if children are to make any progress in musical activities. For the purpose of analysis skills are often classified as 'aural', 'translative' and 'manipulative'. In practice most recognized skills are a combination of abilities. Sight singing, for example requires people to be able to sing in tune (aural), read notation (translative) and control the voice (manipulative).

A crucial question facing teachers (and curriculum planners) is how *much* emphasis should be placed on the development of skills in a programme of class music lessons. One of the great disputes amongst music educators, over many years, has centred on the issue as to whether or not pupils should be taught musical literacy skills. A typical example of this controversy is to be found in conflicting articles by Aelwyn Pugh[5] and Malcolm Pointon.[6] Pugh argues that literacy skill (defined as the ability to convert musical sound into signs, and musical signs into sounds) is fundamental to musical understanding and development. Musical autonomy is dependent on musical literacy.

In contrast, Pointon states that much of today's music cannot be notated in standard form; in fact, two thirds of the world's music is not notated anyway. Rather than increasing understanding, Pointon claims that musical literacy can actually inhibit exploration, response and creative insight. In other words musical literacy becomes a hindrance to the development of musical understanding.

Whether or not the promotion of musical literacy should be a curriculum aim depends on the underlying conception of music education being adopted. Whilst Pointon makes some strong points against the teaching of literacy skills it has to be acknowledged that children in this country are being educated in, and for, a society in which a large proportion of music is notated. An ability to use standard notation is therefore a necessary skill or tool. Those who adopt the principles of Curwen and Kodaly place much emphasis on musical literacy. But the acquisition of these skills is not simply for the purpose of being able to 'read notes'; it is part of a system of aural training designed to develop 'inner hearing' — a basic musical operation. Quite clearly, inner hearing is not necessarily dependent on musical literacy. In oral/aural cultures people display highly sophisticated musical operations. But in *our* society there is a strong *connection* between musical literacy and musical thinking. And it is interesting to observe that educators who dismiss musical literacy as being unnecessary are usually those who rely on it all the time!

It is certainly the case that if aural, translative or manipulative abilities are given undue attention, and taught as ends rather than means, music programmes can become dull, mechanical and devoid of any artistic joy; under these circumstances interest in music is obviously likely to wane. However, one of the reasons why many children become uninterested in music may be that they develop little skill. In an interesting investigation into the attitudes of a group of secondary school pupils, David Grierson[7] found substantial evidence which would lend support to this view. For these pupils, who had acquired few skills, music had become a closed subject. All practical activities appeared to remain at the same 'level'; the pupils felt that lack of technique prevented them from making any real progress in music. (It is worth comparing these findings with the pupils' comments quoted in Chapter 5).

Musical skills are necessary insofar as they enable pupils to participate in activities through which musical understanding is realized. This will apply even at a very elementary level. A child playing simple tunes by rote on a xylophone must at least know how to manipulate the beaters and be able to recognize and remember a pattern of sounds. In curriculum planning and practice what needs to be established is the necessary relationship between musical skills and activities. However, one of the main problems in the teaching of literacy and other skills is that the learning conditions are often far from ideal. I shall return to this point in the next chapter.

Subject Matter

According to the Gulbenkian Foundation's report, *The Arts in Schools*,[8] many people seem to be under the impression that schools have the reponsibility of passing on 'high' art to their pupils. There is a common view, that arts education is, or should be, a matter of simply introducing children to the 'best' of the culture. It is extremely doubtful if there are many teachers who would see music education quite in these terms. Certainly, a curriculum programme concerned with music of the great European composers *alone* would reflect a very narrow conception of music education. Nevertheless, the European 'classical' tradition is a highly significant constituent of the world of music as we know it; *part* of being introduced to that world is to become acquainted with some of the works of major composers. However, there are educators who maintain that for a large number of children the classical tradition has little relevance.

This sort of attitude is to be found in the writings of Christopher Small.[9] He argues that members of the musical establishment have generally accepted the post-Renaissance 'concert hall' tradition of high-art music as the zenith of musical achievement. In so doing musicians have overlooked the variety, richness and significance of music from non-western cultures. Small is concerned to illustrate how in Western societies music has become 'stultified' as a result of concentration on 'consumption' rather than 'creative processes'. His very interesting references to traditional African and Balinese cultures are used to indicate how music in those societies is part of everyday life. In western societies music has become remote and virtually irrelevant to large numbers of the population.

Small's sharp critique of western musical values is extremely thought-provoking; many of his observations have contributed to a reappraisal of the content of music education programmes. But how far the notion of relevance can be a suitable criterion for the selection of curriculum content is highly questionable. Certainly, a great deal of music is not relevant in the sense of its being part of childrens' immediate environment, as it might be in a pre-industrial society, However, the very essence of education, and particularly in the arts, is the idea of transporting people to worlds beyond their daily experiences. In our society, whether we like it or not, there is a sense in which music exists 'out there'; but it does not follow that such music is therefore irrelevant. The notion of relevance as a criterion for the selection of curriculum content is, in fact, very dubious and fraught with difficulties. Of course, teachers have to make decisions about the suitability of particular materials. But the great danger of deciding that the classical tradition as a whole is not relevant to pupils is of denying them access to an area of knowledge and experience which is central to our musical culture. In a system where equality of opportunity is regarded as a right it is very hard to see how such a course of action can possibly be defended on educational grounds. The reality of practice is that when children do respond positively to a particular song or an orchestral work, whatever its style or genre, questions of relevance seldom seem to arise. Nobody said in 1990 that *Nessun dorma* was irrelevant; people just liked it as a piece of music.

Related to this idea of relevance is the view that curricula should reflect children's interests. In some cases this represents a child-centred theory of education; in others the principle is based on a 'reconstructionist' approach to music itself. Both of these positions appear in the various writings of Graham Vulliamy,[10] who claims that teachers have tended to adopt a narrow view as to what 'counts' as music within an educational context. There has, in fact, been an important musical 'revolution' marked by developments in Afro-American styles resulting in the 'legitimization' of a 'new musical language'. Vulliamy maintains that music education practices have been dominated by the methods and techniques of the European 'serious' tradition. As a more appropriate alternative he proposes an 'open' style of music education in which pupils would be engaged in self-directed work based on their interests in various types of popular music. Pupils might not necessarily read music but will learn to play by listening to recordings or by following the examples of friends in the class. Working in this way many pupils who would not otherwise be regarded as musical may achieve considerable musical satisfaction.

Vulliamy's observations on music educators' prejudiced attitudes towards popular music, during the 1960s and 1970s, are fully justified. There was a tendency to dismiss any popular music as 'commercial rubbish' which should be avoided at all costs in educational programmes; this was certainly a very biased and unwarranted perspective. Nevertheless a scheme of music education based largely on children's interests in popular music could become just as narrow, in terms of content, as the traditional curriculum of which Vulliamy is rightly critical. Again, there is always the danger of pupils being denied opportunities to experience other types of music and forms of music making. This is not to imply that popular music should not feature on the curriculum. Most pupils are probably interested in popular styles and this may be one good reason for including them in a music programme. But apart from this, children and adults respond to the many types of popular music *as music*. It has its own significance and value and can take its place alongside other forms. In fact, Vulliamy has edited two splendid books which are not only extremely informative about styles of popular music but also provide some excellent suggestions for classroom practice.[11]

The general problem with educating interests is twofold. Firstly, it is taken for granted that teachers always know what children's interests are at any given time. As I have said, it is likely that most children are interested in popular music, but anybody who teaches in school will know that many have other musical interests. If a child says, 'I am interested in sixteenth century polyphony', do we then base his programme on the works of Palestrina and Vittoria? There seldom seems to be any clear and convincing answer to this type of question. Secondly, education is concerned with providing children with *new* interests, *new* experiences, *new* visions. To educate children is to free them from what is often a very limited view of the world. A programme based entirely on popular music would hardly seem to be the way of achieving such an aim.

Denis Lawton's frequently quoted definition of the curriculum as being a 'selection from the culture'[12] raises the point that we live in a multi-cultural society. Many educators have argued that more consideration should be given to this factor when planning the content of music and arts curricula.[13] Certainly the questioning of the supremacy of the Post-Renaissance tradition by sociologists and ethnomusicologists is a timely reminder that this tradition is by no means the entire world of music; in a pluralist society there is undoubtedly justification for representing more than what is (mistakenly) called the mainstream culture on the curriculum. There is a rich variety of music of many different styles which is valued in our present society; to ignore this is to overlook the possibilities of wider musical experience.

But it is important to avoid treating the issue of arts education in, and for, a multi-cultural society in a superficial manner. Selecting forms of Indian, Chinese or African music to satisfy the needs of ethnic groups is simply a crude tokenism and can easily result in alienation and segregation. John Blacking[14] makes the point that much talk about 'multicultural' education is misinformed and potentially dangerous. Children in this country are being educated for *this* society and ideas about an education suited to particular ethnic minorities can, in fact, place such groups at a disadvantage. Blacking favours the study of world musics but for *musical* rather than social reasons:

> The serious study of world arts in schools could be a distinctive British characteristic of arts education in the United Kingdom; it would recognize the varied cultural

origins of the country's citizens and the many life-styles that co-exist, while at the same time stimulating a sense of national unity by a common interest in artistic exploration and experience. The presence of African and Asian arts has value in the context of the European Great tradition because they are novel and technically different systems. If, however, they are promoted for social reasons, simply because there are persons of African and Asian origin living in this country, their value is immediately debased.[15]

The task for music teachers is to devise practical activities which involve children in the wide variety of music that is part not only of this society but also the 'world' society. Some of the most thoughtful and fruitful innovations in this area have been introduced by music educators who have concentrated on making *connections* between different musical genres. The work of Jack Dobbs, Frances Shepherd[16] and Robert Kwami[17] is particularly notable. Whilst drawing attention to the importance of identifying and respecting cultural traditions and conventions, they have shown how a focus on musical 'similarities' can become a basis for broadening the music curriculum. This approach is in keeping with Blacking's ethnomusicological view that musics (and other art forms) ultimately transcend culture.[18] Blacking argues that this is because there are 'deep' musical structures in all music which are related to common human experiences. Stylistic variations between musics of different cultures are essentially to do with surface features. (This is very similar to Howard Gardner's position discussed in the previous chapter).

The 'official' approval given to the performing-composing-listening paradigm has also been extended to the principle that all pupils should experience a wide range of musical styles, forms and genres. In the London and East Anglian Group GCSE syllabus, for example, it is stated that candidates will be required to 'identify and demonstrate their awareness of music of the past and present in relation to (a) Western European styles and trends, (b) Afro-American styles, trends and idioms, (c) traditions other than (a) and (b).[19] Since the GCSE is not only a new examination, but also a major curriculum development initiative with implications for practice at all stages of education, this policy is likely to be seen as having a wider applicability. But obviously children cannot come into contact with every musical style and genre; principles have to be interpreted in a flexible manner. When the GCSE was first introduced many teachers expressed concern over the range of music they would be expected to include in their curricula and their lack of knowledge of music from non-Western cultures. No one can be an *expert* in every field; as always music teachers are required to be general practitioners.

The emphasis on broad musical experience is indicative of changing attitudes towards music as an art form. These newer perspectives reflect the influence of musicians, sociologists and ethnomusicologists who, in challenging certain established assumptions, have extended musical horizons. Related to these broader conceptions of music is an increasing awareness of, and commitment to, the notion of music as one of a community of disciplines united by a common mode of perceptual and imaginative understanding. In many schools music staff no longer work in isolation; they are members of arts faculties.

Music and Combined Arts Programmes

For some years there has been a continuous debate over the advantages and disadvantages of teaching music within the context of an *arts* curriculum. There is frequent reference to topics such as integration, inter-disciplinary inquiry, multi-disciplinary projects and inter-related activities. It is not unusual for these various terms to be used in a fairly loose manner; this sometimes leads to confusion and misunderstanding.[20] Many teachers have been involved in initiatives designed to bring the arts together. However, one has only to attend a conference or meeting of arts teachers to realize that opinion can be very divided regarding the educational value and practical efficiency of this type of curriculum organization.

Underlying controversies surrounding combined arts programmes there exists a philosophical view about the nature of the arts. Whilst some educators and artists wish to emphasize common and therefore uniting elements, others concentrate on the distinct features of the separate disciplines and the differences between them. Whatever the theoretical justification for, or objection to, the establishment of combined curricula, such moves might also be seen as a means of improving the status of the arts in schools. However, the grouping of subjects could also be regarded as an attempt to cut resources and 'water down' the arts; this would obviously lower their status. Consequently, any consideration of combined programmes raises questions not only about the nature of the arts and artistic experience, but also about the social and political factors that affect the organization of knowledge within educational institutions.

A central and often highly contentious issue in this whole debate is the concept of integration. In a famous paper on the selection and distribution of knowledge in schools, Basil Bernstein distinguishes between what he calls a 'collection code' curriculum and an 'integrated' curriculum.[21] The former arises when curriculum subjects are separated whilst the latter results from the removal of traditional subject barriers. These organizational patterns are referred to as the 'classification' of knowledge; this can be either 'strong' (collection code) or 'weak' (integrated). Bernstein also introduces the concept of 'framing' in order to characterize pedagogical style. With strong framing the teacher is the authority who imparts knowledge; weak framing allows for greater negotiation between teachers and pupils. Bernstein maintains that the way in which knowledge is perceived and organized in an institution reveals something of its power structure. Those who seek to safeguard their academic territory and preserve the *status quo* will tend to favour strong classification and strong framing; those who are concerned to break down academic and social barriers will incline towards weaker forms of both classification and framing.

Although Bernstein is talking about curricula in general it is not hard to see how his analysis can be applied specifically to arts curricula. The Head of, say, an established and thriving music department may well be unhappy about losing his identity in a larger arts consortium. Leaving aside how moving from one type of organization to another might bring about changes in curriculum content and pedagogical style, it will almost certainly have some effect on the teacher's professional status within the school. Integration might be seen, therefore, as a good or bad thing according to how it affects teachers both personally and professionally. To be the Head of an integrated arts department could be professionally advantageous; to be simply a member of such a department might not be so appealing.

This sort of argument is at a theoretical level. It would be most unwise to infer that supporters and opponents of integrated arts curricula are necessarily involved in some type of power game. But I think this social dimension of integration is often ignored in current arts education reviews. We know little about the different sorts of reasons and motives which lead people to support either subject-based or integrated curricula. On the whole the focus of attention has been on philosophical and pedagogical issues.

At a conference organized by the National Association for Education in the Arts in 1984 the motion debated was 'We believe that teaching the arts in an integrated way is the most effective for both teacher and taught'.[22] One important point which emerges from subsequent articles by Richard Addison[23] and Dorothy Taylor[24] is the variety of ways in which the term integration is used. This is well illustrated in an earlier paper by Richard Pring,[25] who shows how an analysis of integration leads to a consideration of different epistemological issues. There is, according to Pring, a philosophical tradition which emphasizes the unity of all knowledge 'such that the meaning of one proposition cannot be grasped without an implicit reference to an entire system of propositions'.[26] Pring's concern is with the whole curriculum, but there has grown up the idea of 'art' as a 'unified whole'. This is not merely a collection of arts disciplines but a separate 'form'.[27] However, exactly what this form is and how it can become a model for arts curricula is far from clear. For Addison the arts are unified through a common 'functional language' which is an indicator of an 'art-mode-of-thinking'. The notion of common language through the use of terms like shape, space, line, sequence, weight, etc., is often pointed to as a unifying factor. It is true that these terms are used across the arts in the processes of making, presenting, responding and evaluating. But it is these processes, not the language of terms, which unite the different arts disciplines. In each discipline, or symbolic field, the terminology has a particular meaning. Sometimes the words are used technically; on other occasions they are metaphors.

Tom Gamble,[28] who is well-known to music teachers for his highly imaginative approach to creative work in the secondary school, has expressed strong reservations over attempts to integrate music with other arts subjects. He maintains that this trend has often resulted from an uncritical acceptance of modernist theories and practices. Gamble recognizes the connections between the disciplines but chooses to focus on 'inter-related' arts schemes as a more suitable form of curriculum organization. Personally, I think there is much to be said in favour of this view. Rather than thinking of the arts as 'unified' it may be more practical to consider them as united by what Wittgenstein called 'a complicated network of similarities overlapping and criss-crossing; sometimes overall similarities, sometimes similarities of detail'.[29] What unites the arts is that they are all powerful manifestations of the aesthetic realm of meaning and understanding. As Dewey maintained, the aesthetic is not confined to the arts (anymore than the intellectual is confined to the sciences). But it is in the arts disciplines that the aesthetic is the fundamental mode of operation. For all their obvious differences the arts constitute a unique 'family' of symbolic forms in which 'our ideas of beauty, grace, harmony, balance, harshness, stridency and ugliness are *conceived, formulated* and *expressed*' (*The Arts in Schools*,[30] my italics). This is the characteristic feature of artistic discourse. To recognize their 'overall similarities' is not to advocate teaching the arts as a single form. But it does establish them as a group or community of disciplines and this clearly has a number of practical implications for curriculum planning, organization and practice.

To what extent combined arts projects and programmes in schools actually start from a fully worked out theoretical position is difficult to say. Very often it is teams of teachers, sharing a common commitment and a wish to work together, who are responsible for these initiatives. If individual teachers are not convinced of the value of combined programmes then attempts to introduce or impose them are likely to founder. But there are so many obvious connections between the disciplines that it would surely be highly desirable for teachers to see how the study of a topic in one area could be related and linked to study in another. Such connections are likely to enhance the learning in the separate disciplines. However programmes are finally organized I suggest that there is much to be said for much more collaborative curriculum planning between arts teachers. This is one good reason for organizing arts subjects within a faculty structure.

Some Conclusions

If pupils are to receive a broad and balanced form of music education they will need to follow a curriculum which provides for a range of practical experience and exposure to different musical styles and genres. I have argued that the aim of music education is not to promote musical connoisseurship; rather it is to initiate pupils into a form of life. This will involve the development of skills and procedures that will enable pupils to gain a progressive understanding of music as a realm of meaning. And it is from within this realm that people make aesthetic judgements and come to value music as an art form.

Consequently, there is a strong case for saying that performing, composing and listening activities should form the core of curriculum programmes, for it is through these three experiential modes that children's musical intelligence is released and nurtured. Whether or not *all* programmes should always be based on this principle is another matter. In practice, choice of activities will be determined by a number of variables: the age of pupils, accommodation, time allocation, resources, staffing. All of these factors, and many more, will influence the *actual* operation of curricula. What is absolutely imperative in musical encounters is the quality of experience. Pupils might be composing their own pieces, singing songs, listening to performances or playing instruments in ensembles. But whatever the activity it will need to be stimulating and meaningful and in accordance with the procedures of the discipline. It is in this way that children come to experience the beauty in music and learn to approach activities with a growing sense of competence, precision and artistry. I think there is a great danger, at the present time, of our getting so wrapped up in the 'logic' of curriculum content that the qualitative aspects of educational transactions will be overlooked. Of course, we can write or talk about quality and even emphasize it in curriculum documents; achieving it in practice is another matter. However well planned and documented curriculum specifications might be, their effective implementation is entirely dependent on the actions of teachers. Teaching and learning are complex processes which require careful examination and ultimately some form of empirical study. I shall consider these issues further in the following two chapters.

Notes and References

1   A comment from a pupil in a secondary school recorded by TEE SOOK LENG (1984) *Choirs in Secondary schools. A Study of Pupils Attitudes.* Unpublished M.A. Dissertation, Institute of Education, University of London.

2   WHITE, J. (1973) *Towards a Compulsory Curriculum*, London, Routledge, p. 41.

3   Interesting introspective accounts of creativity are to be found in VERNON, P. (1970) *Creativity*, Harmondsworth, Penguin.
      See also BENNETT, S. (1976) 'The Process of Musical Creation', *Journal of Resarch in Music Education*, *24*, 1, pp. 3–31.

4   MURPHY, W. (1968) 'Creative Music Making in the Primary School', in RAINBOW, B. (Ed.) *Music Teachers Handbook*, London, Novello.

5   PUGH, A. (1980) 'In Defence of Musical Literacy,' *Cambridge Journal of Education*, *10*, 1, pp. 29–34.

6   POINTON, M. (1980) 'Mucking about with noises', A reply to Aelwyn Pugh, *Cambridge Journal of Education*, *10*, 1, pp. 35–39.

7   GRIERSON, D. (1980) 'An Investigation into some factors affecting the attitudes of a group of thirteen-year-old children towards music', Unpublished M.A. Dissertation, Institute of Education University of London.

8   CALOUST GULBENKIAN FOUNDATION (1982) *The Arts in Schools*, p. 36, London, Gulbenkian Foundation.

9   SMALL, C. (1977) *Music — Society — Education*, London, John Calder.

10 VULLIAMY, G. (1977) 'Music as a Case Study in the New Sociology of Education', in SHEPHERD, J. *Whose Music? A Sociology of Musical Languages*, London, Latimer.

11 VULLIAMY, G. and LEE, E. (Eds) (1976) *Pop Music in Schools*, Cambridge, Cambridge University Press.
    VULLIAMY, G. and LEE, E. (Eds) (1982) *Pop, Rock and Ethnic Music*, Cambridge, Cambridge University Press.

12 LAWTON, D. (1989) *Education, Culture and the National Curriculum*, London, Hodder and Stoughton.

13 KHAN, N. (1976) *The Arts Britain Ignores*, London, Community Relations Commission.

14 BLACKING, J. (1986) *Culture and the Arts*, London, National Association for Education in the Arts.

15 *Ibid.*, p. 18.

16 DOBBS, J. and SHEPHERD, F. (1984) 'Music', in CRAFT, A. and BARDELL, G. (Eds) *Curriculum Opportunities in A Multi-Cultural Society*, London, Harper and Row.

17 KWAMI, R. (1986) 'A West African Folktale in the Classroom, *British Journal of Music Education*, *3*, 1, pp. 5–18.

18 BLACKING, J. (1973) *How Musical is Man?* London, Faber.

19 London and East Anglian Group (1990) *Music Syllabus for GCSE.*

20 A good discussion on how these different terms are used is provided by the Central Team of the School Curriculum Development Committee's project, The Arts in Schools. SCDC (1988) *Combined Arts in Secondary Schools.*

21 BERNSTEIN, B. (1971) 'On the Classification and Framing of Knowledge', in YOUNG, M.F.D., *Knowledge and Control: New Directions for the Sociology of Knowledge*, London, Collier-Macmillan.

22 The first NAEA Congress, July 1984.
23 ADDISON, R. (1986) '*The Arts in Education*', Arts Initiatives 1, National Association for Education in the Arts.
24 TAYLOR, D. (1986) 'Integration in the Arts', Arts Initiatives 1, National Association for Education in the Arts.
25 PRING, R.A. (1975) 'Curriculum Integration' in PETERS, R.S. *The Philosophy of Education*, Oxford, Oxford University Press.
26 *Ibid.*, p. 148.
27 See ALLEN, D. (1988) *Models of Combined Arts Practice*, in SCDC (1988) *op. cit.*
28 GAMBLE, T. (1982) 'Music and the integration of the arts', in PAYNTER, J., *Music in the Secondary School Curriculum*, Cambridge, Cambridge University Press.
29 WITTGENSTEIN, L. (1953) *Philosophical Investigations*, London, Blackwell, p. 32.
30 GULBENKIAN FOUNDATION (1982) *op. cit.*, p. 18.
31 SCHOOLS COUNCIL (1981) *The Practical Curriculum*, London, Methuen.

Chapter 4

Teaching and Learning

Introduction

Much has been written about the various 'methods' of music teaching developed over the past 150 years. Curwen, Kodaly, Orff and Dalcroze stand out as major educators who formulated approaches to teaching as part of an overall system of music education. The principles established by these 'Great Music Educators' have been highly influential and continue to command respect; for some teachers they have almost become articles of faith. My intention, in this chapter, is to focus on what I shall call the *conditions* of teaching. These conditions will be relevant, although in different ways, to any single method.

In recent years some child-centred theorists have urged that more emphasis be placed on *learning* and less on teaching. R. Murray Schafer, for example, in a stimulating book on music education, suggests that 'there are no more teachers; there is just a community of learners'.[1] But what are we to understand by this rather enigmatic statement? It is certainly quite right to emphasise the importance of the teacher as a learner, as well as an instructor. However, on occasion one might easily gain the impression that the apparent shift from teaching to learning is to imply that the former somehow inhibits the latter. If teaching is *preventing* learning then there is surely something wrong with the teaching. The point is that the two concepts are, in fact, inter-related and inter-dependent. Essentially, teaching is a series of intentional activities, the aim of which is to bring about learning, and the *quality, style and content* of those activities determine their worth in an educational context.

I shall concentrate on four main issues. First, music teachers are obviously required to have a certain expertise in order to initiate children into forms of musical behaviour and the ways of musical thinking. But teaching is never a matter of developing skills and imparting knowledge in a routine manner. It also involves the transmission of values; these are both implicit and explicit in a teacher's actions and attitudes. For as well as being an instructor and facilitator the teacher is also a *model* for learners. This necessary condition will apply to any form of teaching whatever the subject area. However, for a number of reasons the importance of this condition in the teaching of music is sometimes given only scant attention.

Secondly, there has been much debate recently about the advisability of organizing teaching and learning in accordance with principles derived from either the *objectives* or *process* models of curriculum. Arguments and disagreements which were so prominent twenty years ago have been revived and highlighted by the style of the National Curriculum with its 'target' orientation. There are controversies here which require examination with specific reference to music and musical activity.

The third issue is closely related to the second. It is concerned with the question of how teaching and learning episodes might be sequenced so as to ensure that pupils develop some sense of progressive achievement. This is clearly an important condition but one which can very easily be oversimplified.

Finally, there is the question of pupil assessment. As a result of changing educational policies teachers of all subjects have been forced to give greater attention to this aspect of their professional work. It is recognized that assessment is directly related to teaching and learning, but there is anxiety over the complexity of new strategies and the amount of time required for assessment exercises. There is also uncertainty and some justified suspicion about how assessment data might be used.

Teacher as Authority and Model

I have argued that the central aim of music education is to engage pupils in practical activities through which they will come to learn and internalize the procedures of the discipline. In this way they develop musical thinking and a sense of *musicianship*. Procedures have to be taught — pupils need to be shown and told what to do — but there is also an important sense in which they are 'caught'. A distinctive feature of musical learning is that people come to understand the methods, or procedures, of music by working with others who are already on the inside of the discipline. This happens particularly in corporate activities: choirs, bands, ensemble groups. The 'initiates' assume the role of models; they demonstrate a form of behaviour in musical pursuits which is gradually assimilated, often quite unconsciously by the novices. A similar situation arises in the classroom, but here it is the teacher who is the model. Therefore, the onus is very much on the music teacher to exhibit appropriate musical behaviour, or musicianship, in his pedagogy. In this way he establishes the right 'setting' for musical activity; musical learning can only really occur in a proper musical environment.

The idea of the teacher as a model is emphasized in the well-known instructional theory of Robert Gagne.[2] He draws attention to the fact that the development of pupils' attitudes towards a particular activity or subject will be largely determined by the attitudes and behaviour of the teacher. The same point is to be found in the writings of Bruner; referring to his theory of instruction Dorothy Taylor proposes that the music teacher should:

> ... pave the way for the learner's aesthetic response and musical feeling by his own behaviour as a musician.... Ideally he must perform the simplest song with the same care, musicianship and sense of occasion as he would a Beethoven violin sonata.[3]

Of course, this does not mean that the teacher has to be a virtuoso performer, and in any case, the teaching of music involves much more than a mere 'display' of musicianship. Dr. Taylor is emphasizing an attitude towards music teaching, and most teachers would probably agree with her observation. So often in curriculum development projects, and in *writings* about

the practice of music education, this aspect of teaching is overlooked or, at least, not fully acknowledged.

During the past few years there has been an accelerating
growth of new methods, guidelines, classroom materials and
various items of equipment designed to assist teachers in their
work. These developments are to be welcomed; much of the
new material is highly imaginative and attractive. Many of the
available music packages have been produced with the needs of
the so-called non-specialist in mind. Teachers who regard themselves as in this category will be constantly looking for ideas and
support materials. But it is very regrettable that in attempting to
promote music in schools through the development of materials
some innovators have inadvertently ignored certain basic conditions of teaching in general and music teaching in particular.

This was apparent in the Schools Council Project *Music
Education for Young Children*, originally intended for general class
teachers who were 'lacking in confidence' about music and
might even be 'musically illiterate'.[4] Packs of materials were
produced which (it was claimed) could be used by these teachers
for the purpose of setting up musical activities in the classroom.
One aim was to develop pupils' musical literacy skills. The
materials were seen as an 'in-service course' for teachers who
could learn 'alongside' the pupils.

However, two fundamental points about teaching music
were completely misrepresented. First, even in the teaching of
the most elementary skills it is necessary for the teacher to
demonstrate to pupils and make a series of evaluative judgements about their responses and progress. When young children
clap a simple rhythm pattern, for example, it is seldom, if ever,
a matter of 'right' or 'wrong'. Teachers must be able to decide
on the 'rightness' or 'wrongness' of pupils' actions, spot particular difficulties, provide corrective information, encourage
musicality and steer pupils along a suitable path. This is no
mechanical process. In order to do all of these things the teacher
must have a secure grasp of the skill; it can never be learned
'alongside' the pupils be listening to a series of tape recordings
or reading the teacher's support book. It is a purely logical point
that the teacher needs to be *an authority* in relation to the learner.

Secondly, activities such as class singing or instrumental performance will only become properly meaningful if conducted in a musical manner; that is, in accordance with the correct procedural principles. Teaching a song, for example, is far more than just getting pupils to sing the right notes. It involves demonstrating phrasing, dynamics, style and expressive nuances. Teachers need to understand technical points and difficulties. They have to be in a position to decide on suitable learning strategies in order to assist pupils over particular hurdles. These techniques are normally taken for granted, and require a certain musical expertise and experience. Unless the teacher has that necessary expertise, which is acquired over a period of time through musical engagement, it is impossible to see how any meaningful teaching can take place. All music teaching calls for subtle and refined musical judgement. To think that a person can rely entirely on books, materials or instruction manuals to provide the basis of an adequate pedagogy is quite mistaken. Indeed, as Kodaly always insisted, teaching is not only a skilful but also an artistic activity; it depends on the individual being able to transform materials and bring them to life in encounters with children.

As a result of moves in the primary sector to either dispense with the services of music specialists or re-define their role, many generalist class teachers are finding themselves in the position of having to teach music. Consequently, they are looking for advice and courses for the 'non-specialist'. There are published schemes available which can be used effectively by teachers who have limited musical expertise and there is an increasing amount of valuable INSET work in this area. However, it is wrong to assume that because generalists can teach most curriculum subjects they can automatically teach music if they have guides and support materials. They may be able 'to cope' and *contribute* to children's musical education in this way, particularly in a school where there is a music 'consultant', or co-ordinator, who can guide and direct the main programme, but if music is to be a truly meaningful and dynamic part of children's education then the foundations of musical understanding must be firmly laid in the early years of schooling. This is an issue which is being sadly neglected at the present time; in many cases children are often getting no more than a mere glimpse of music.

Although a certain degree of musical competence can be regarded as a necessary condition for teaching the subject there is a further and, indeed, essential condition. Music teachers are required to have a particular attitude towards music as a discipline. It is the attitude of the practising *musician* and may be contrasted with that of the musical 'enthusiast'. There can be a significant difference. The enthusiast may have wide or narrow interests. However, *as* an enthusiast he can pick and choose according to his preferences. But the musician, although he too will have personal preferences, has a commitment to a form of life. His approach to music over-rides his preferences. This is usually referred to as a sense of 'professionalism'; it has been aptly exemplified by Sir Adrian Boult when he says:

> It has always been my chief object to perform everything as if it were the finest piece of music I have ever known. It follows that I can have no favourites.[5]

Practising musicians will fully appreciate Sir Adrian's point; it is one that has a direct bearing on the teaching of music in both primary and secondary schools and particularly in relation to the content of the curriculum.

Part of the procedure of music is to value the music being used in a particular activity. If a person does not value, say, certain popular styles or *avant garde* works and takes no delight in non-Western musics, will he be able to introduce these forms to pupils with enthusiasm and a genuine sense of commitment? I think it is most unlikely. In fact, it may well be that programmes are often determined by teachers' personal tastes in music. But this cannot be a very suitable basis for music *education*. I have argued in favour of the policy of introducing pupils to a wide range of musical styles and traditions. This is not for social reasons; it is not for the purpose of satisfying the 'needs' or 'interests' of minority groups. The argument hinges on the principle of initiating pupils into the world of music in all its diversity, this being the central aim of music education. The development of a broad curriculum is not simply a matter of *selecting* a variety of content. It is very much dependent on the teacher's musical perspective and commitment to the *discipline* of music. I think it is most important to establish the principle of the teacher not only as a musical authority but also as a musician who approaches his art as a professional practitioner. Both of these factors are necessary conditions for the conduct of music programmes. They also have implications for the education and training of music teachers. I shall pursue these issues further in Chapter 6.

Objectives and Processes

Music teachers have often been criticized for not specifying clearly defined goals in their curriculum schemes and programmes of study. However, the need to work towards objectives has for long been considered to be one of the requirements of effective class music teaching. In his report on music in secondary schools (1922), Dr. Arthur Somervell,[6] a distinguished musician and the senior HMI for music, expressed some disappointment over the way the subject was being taught; only 'limited progress' had been made in the development of music curricula. He particularly regretted the fact that few teachers had a definite syllabus with statements of *objectives*. It seems incontrovertible that any form of teaching, because of its *intentional* nature, must be directed towards some goals or stated ends. But the issue of objectives in education has become one of the most bitterly disputed topics in modern times. What has made it so is the impact of the *behavioural objectives model* of curriculum.

The origins of the model can be traced back to the development of American industrial systems during the early years of this century.[7] Nowadays, one of the most frequently cited statements of its underlying principles and structure is Ralph Tyler's famous book *Basic Principles of Curriculum and Instruction*.[8] Tyler's celebrated rationale is based on the premise that any curriculum design must begin with a clear specification of objectives, or 'intended learning outcomes'. These are to be derived from a number of sources (philosophy, psychology, sociology, subject matter) and formulated in terms of precise 'pupil behaviours'. This 'classical' objectives model has a persuasive logic and clarity, but it also represents a view of educational practice which many teachers find unrealistic and unacceptable.

One objection to the model is that it presupposes an oversimplified and essentially mistaken idea regarding the function of curriculum theories. According to Tyler and others, curriculum theory is prescriptive or recommendatory and precedes the practice of teaching. On this view, good practice is dependent on the identification of objectives and detailed planning of schemes of work and individual lessons. Critics argue, and I believe the argument to be entirely justified, that whilst planning is obviously necessary, effective pedagogy is far more complicated than simply getting things 'right' at the planning stage. A second type of criticism is that there would be many important educational objectives that could never be stated in precise behavioural terms. To appreciate works of art would be a typical example. An objective such as 'pupils should be able to demonstrate an appreciation of Beethoven's Seventh Symphony' is thoroughly admirable as an ideal; but the identification of the objective in terms of overt pupil behaviour is highly problematic. How could one ever really decide on what would *count* as appreciative behaviour?

A strong argument against *teaching* to defined objectives is that the practice of education seldom operates in this predetermined way. Professor Richard Pring, a staunch opponent of the model, has frequently maintained that educational activities do not allow teachers to state, in advance, exactly what the outcomes will be.[9] According to Pring, as soon as one is taking part in an activity the original objectives *change*. This is because those involved, that is teachers and pupils, are thinking, autonomous individuals who interact with each other in such a way — if the activity is genuinely educational — so as to make the statement of outcomes logically impossible. People ask questions, make comments, seek clarification; there is a constant exchange of ideas and information. This is not to suggest that lessons should be casual or undirected in style; but the course of educational encounters will be decided by the procedures and processes of the discipline into which pupils are being introduced, with an emphasis on what it is to act and think in a particular way: historically, mathematically, scientifically, musically. It is this conception of teaching and learning, with the focus on 'quality' of educational experience, which is at the heart of the process model of curriculum.

Now it might be held that those who favour the process model do so because of their interest in particular curriculum subjects and fields of inquiry. Indeed, one suspects that the arguments put forward by opponents of the objectives model are closely related to teaching in areas such as Social Studies which will include a large amount of group and class discussion. Worthwhile educational discussion would be characterized not by the realization of particular learning outcomes, but by the emphasis on procedures — the acceptance of evidence, respect for alternative viewpoints, a commitment to objectivity.

It is not hard to conceive of certain types of music lessons where stated objectives may be quickly forgotten as a result of questions raised, points discussed and interests shared. Even in old-style 'class singing lessons', which if properly organized will be carefully structured and seemingly amenable to clearly stated objectives, it is not at all uncommon for teachers to deviate from the original plan. Presumably, for the hard-line objectives theorist this would be seen as unsatisfactory. However, in practice it would be rather strange to refer to a lesson as being educationally unsuccessful or unproductive simply because the pupils did not realize the pre-stated objectives whatever these might have been. To do so would be to use inappropriate criteria for what counts as a successful lesson. The sorts of questions to be asked would be: Were the pupils involved in worthwhile musical activities? Did they learn things which were relevant (although not previously stated) to the general aims of the programme? Were they participating in a positive way and with a sense of enthusiasm? Did they display some sense of artistry and expressive style in their work? In other words, the criteria of judgement would be more to do with the qualitative aspects of the educational transaction rather than the achievement of some initially stated outcome. Indeed, it is not at all unusual for teachers to say that a lesson 'went well' but did not turn out as predicted.

Nevertheless, it would be peculiar if *all* lessons followed this pattern of events and none of the stated objectives were ever realized. In a programme of music education certain things do have to be achieved; songs must be learned, skills have to be acquired, performances must be given, compositions need to be completed. It is the realization of such objectives that actually constitutes some of the procedures of the discipline. But talking of an objective in this way is to use the term in a far less stipulative manner. Consequently, there is a need to distinguish between objectives as part of a 'common sense' teaching strategy, and *behavioural* objectives which are specified learning outcomes associated with an educational ideology. In fact, it is the failure to make this distinction that has led to so much heated debate over the whole issue.

The common sense version is applicable to the kind of context in which a teacher asks himself the question 'what is the objective of this lesson?' In a typical performance situation, for example, it would be quite in order to say, at the outset, that as a result of instruction pupils 'should be able to present a musical performance of Material One'. The reason for stating an objective in this way does not imply any ideological commitment to the objectives model; neither does it rule out any unexpected encounters. Such a statement merely reflects the nature of musical activity itself; performance activities are necessarily directed towards the realization of an objective, namely, the peformance. Although in a sense this is quite obvious there is, nevertheless, an issue here of some importance. Performance, as it occurs in class lessons, has frequently been taken to mean 'participation'. There is a popular belief that 'taking part in' and not the final outcome (i.e. the performance) is what makes singing or playing educationally significant and worthwhile. This type of attitude might be seen as representing a 'liberal' and less exclusive view of musical activity, but it can also belie a rather specious position. For unless these activities are pursued with the intention of producing a proper performance, one that has a certain aesthetic quality and style, there is no reason why the procedures should be attended to in any more than a perfunctory manner. Class singing lessons which are simply sing-songs may be forms of entertainment or relaxation; some people

call them 'fun' activities, but they have limited value in a programme concerned primarily with the development of a real
musical understanding. It is only by working at music in a way
that links the process with a performance objective that the
activity becomes musically meaningful to the participants.

Another argument against teaching towards a pre-stated,
(even common sense) objective is that in so doing attention is
directed solely to the objective; this is likely to be to the detriment of the quality of the learning experience. Certainly in some
curriculum areas it may well be that pupils do achieve objectives
but with little feeling for, or interest in, the subject matter; this
could arise in the acquisition of musical skills and propositional
knowledge. But the argument cannot be legitimately applied to
objectives in performance simply because the objective will
never be realized unless the process is in accordance with
correct procedural principles. It might also be claimed that a
lesson (or series of lessons) which consisted of good procedure
(or process) but resulted in substandard performance was,
nevertheless, educationally valuable. There is perhaps some substance to this argument. However, when a performance 'goes
wrong' we would normally conclude that insufficient attention
had been given to certain points during the preparation period.
In other words, the final judgement of the process is in terms of
a discernable outcome or product.

This type of thinking about objectives and processes in
performance can also be related to composition. There have,
over the years, been many differences of opinion as to whether
the value of composition lies in the 'process' or the 'product'.
In the previous chapter I maintained that the significance of
compositional activities is to be found in the process whereby
children gain further experience of procedural principles. But
again, unless this process is directed towards the production of
a composition it is difficult, if not impossible, to make sense
of the activity.

Although the *behavioural* objectives model does have certain
pedagogical limitations there will be times when the principles
are likely to be of some relevance; even the most ardent critics of
the model have recognized this.[10] In music teaching the most
obvious example would be skill acquisition. We might state a

behavioural objective, such as 'pupils should be able to play the chords C, F and G on the keyboard'. Learning to play these chords is a specific task; it is only open to discussion insofar as the discussion has a bearing on the acquisition of the skill. A teacher could hardly be accused of acting in an uneducational manner if he prevented discussion which was likely to get in the way of mastering the skill. In this case we can specify quite clearly what it is that pupils should be able to do as a result of instruction. And programmes of music education would probably be much more effective if the teaching of skills was carried out in a more structured and ordered manner.

On one level the objectives and process models of curriculum could be regarded as reflecting different educational ideals. In fact, the former, as conceived by Tyler, represents a comprehensive theory of curriculum; the latter is a reaction to, and rejection of, that theory. From the point of view of pedagogical principles, however, the two models need not be viewed as mutually exclusive. Both can be applied in some way to the various activities that constitute music education practice.

It is also important to distinguish between *behavioural* objectives and *common sense* objectives. The great weakness of the classical model in its original form is that it overlooks the complexity of the teaching and learning interaction. This is what is disturbing about the current emphasis on 'targets'. When one goes into a classroom as a visitor it is always the quality of the educational environment that leads one to conclude that there is either good or bad teaching in progress. Unless the process of teaching and learning is of the right qualitative order then pre-stated outcomes have little meaning or value. It is *how* children learn things that is important.

Sequence and Progression

The concern over objectives in music teaching is closely related to the question of sequence and progression. It has been said that programmes of music education in schools are too frequently lacking in sequential structure; this prevents pupils developing a sense of continuity and progression in the subject. Music teachers in secondary schools know that new entrants have often had very different types of musical experience in their primary schools. Consequently, they sometimes feel obliged to treat all pupils as 'beginners'. Likewise, staff in the primary sector might conclude that on transfer to secondary school some pupils do not always have the opportunities of building on what has been achieved in the early years. Serious attempts are now being made to provide much more co-ordination between secondary schools and the feeder primaries. The current emphasis on the whole curriculum from the ages of 5 to 16 is, in itself, a move towards improved continuity. Quite clearly it is important that a course of music education should be sequenced in a way that ensures pupils acquire a feeling of progressive achievement.

However, the issue is by no means straight forward. Any ideas of sequence as a simple linear progression based on the logical order of subject matter, which in turn becomes the basis for teaching and learning, is to misunderstand and distort the nature of musical experience and musical development. There is an underlying assumption in the objectives model of curriculum (and to some extent in the National Curriculum) that knowledge is hierarchically organized, can be broken down into discrete units and then learned in a systematic manner. How far the learning of something is *ever* in accordance with its logical structure is extremely questionable. But it does not follow that the teaching and learning of curriculum subjects can begin anywhere. A critical question for music educators concerns the implications of the development of musical operations for the structure and sequencing of school programmes?

Some illuminating ideas on this subject are to be found in Bruner's notion of the 'spiral curriculum'.[11] He advocates introducing the essential concepts of a form of knowledge and constantly returning to them in ways appropriate to children's stages of cognitive development. Through this process pupils acquire an understanding of the methods and 'deep structures' of the disciplines. One attempt to apply Bruner's instructional theory to music education is the *Manhattanville Music Curriculum Program*.[12] This scheme is based on the principle that the 'spiral curriculum allows even the beginning student to think, create and explore music in the manner of a musician'.[13] The programme consists of sixteen cycles, each of which is concerned with the development of central musical 'concepts' (dynamics, timbre, form, pitch, rhythm) and skills (dextrous, translative and aural). These are applied through a variety of performing, creative and listening activities. Pupils working at the first level (or cycle) are involved, essentially, in the same *process* as those pupils operating at the higher levels. All this is highly commendable. However, the *Manhattanville Program* suggests the increasing growth of a 'conceptual framework'; the impression given is that growth of musical understanding is similar to growth of, say, scientific understanding; both would depend on the development of concepts and a network of related propositions. Consequently, one feels that Bruner's theory has been applied too readily to music and music teaching. Insufficient thought is given to the substantive differences between *conceptual* knowledge and *perceptual* knowledge. From a *musical* point of view, the spiral curriculum suggests that activities may be regarded as fundamentally the same in *manner* at all stages of development. For example, there is an important sense in which a class singing lesson for young children is exactly the same sort of musical activity as an adult professional choir at rehearsal. Both forms of activity are determined by attention to procedural principles. The basic process of the activity does not change.

Nevertheless, more recent studies of musical intelligence provide convincing evidence to indicate that children pass through stages of development. They will respond to, and interest themselves in, musical phenomena according to their developmental stages. In an interesting investigation based on a detailed analysis of children's compositions, Keith Swanwick and June Tillman[14] hypothesize eight developmental 'modes'. The young child appears to focus on the sensory qualities of music such as timbre and dynamics; older children seek to explore structural possibilities and conventional musical idioms. Swanwick and Tillman conclude that demonstration of different forms of musical representation will have a bearing on the sequencing of teaching and learning episodes.

Part of sequencing activities will naturally involve selecting materials which are appropriate to the age and previous experience of the pupils. Developmental studies suggest that the manner in which subject matter is used governs its suitability for a particular age group. Beethovens's Seventh Symphony, the songs of Schubert and the music of Stockhausen can be meaningful, although in different ways, to pupils of all ages provided the music is presented in a way which takes into account children's stages of development. This is the point Bruner is making when he says:

Any idea or problem or body of knowledge can be presented in a form simple enough so that any particular learner can understand it.[15]

In considering sequencing there may be a natural inclination to think of curricula as becoming ever more 'difficult'. But to make progress in musical pursuits does not mean simply to strive after greater technical competence. Of course, choice of activities and materials will be determined to some extent by pupils' levels of skill. Many materials designed for class use might look straightforward enough to the experienced musician but often require more firmly established techniques than is sometimes realized. There might also be a tendency to place importance only on musical literacy and overlook the significance of other types of skills. Some of the published music for class orchestra, for example, although appropriate for inexperienced players in terms of literacy, does often require that pupils have a certain manipulative proficiency. If popular classroom instruments such as xylophones and electronic keyboards are to be used effectively pupils will need to acquire sufficient techniques. Lack of technical control limits musical progress and often leads to frustration and disappointment.

It is unlikely that conventional musical skills can be developed beyond a fairly elementary level within the context of class lessons. This is because the conditions for skill learning are not favourable. One of the most important conditions is, obviously, practice. Whilst there are differences of opinion regarding its organization, the overwhelming research evidence points to the greater efficiency of distributed practice, that is, practice which is spread out over a period of time. Most instrumentalists and instrumental teachers would probably agree that regular daily practice is essential for the maintenance and development of techniques. If pupils have only one or two timetabled lessons each week it is impossible to arrange schedules which are needed for the effective development of skills.

However, as I have already argued, progress in music education is not solely a matter of children becoming ever more technically competent. Fundamentally, progress consists of their acquiring a growing awareness of the procedures of music through a wide variety of activities and experiences. In these ways musical activity remains a constant source of interest. I agree with John Paynter when he says:

> Each new work (or each fresh performance of a piece already known) should involve a re-thinking of the music in the light of experience gained.[16]

Views about progression in music education tend to be unduly influenced by a musical 'mental state'. It is the notion of the virtuoso performer as the paradigm of musical achievement. This ideal, of course, is manifest in the Grade examinations. Pupils work their way up the ladder of success until they reach Grade 8 or even a diploma. But this model of musical progression is far from appropriate to the organization and practice of music as a curriculum subject. A better model is the interested amateur choralist or orchestral player. This is the person who progresses in music not by getting 'better' in a purely technical sense but by broadening his musical outlook through increased knowledge of repertoire and a range of musical encounters. And if as a result of their experiences in school pupils can eventually see some point in music and musical activity then their progress will be very real indeed. They may never be technically very 'advanced' but this will not prevent them from valuing music as a realm of meaning and form of understanding.

Assessment, Teaching and Learning

Most teachers (although certainly not all) would agree that assessing pupils' work is an important and necessary part of teaching. It is usual practice for teachers to monitor and record pupils' achievements in order to build up a picture of their progress over a period of time. Assessments may be carried out in both formal and informal ways and will be used for the purpose of determining various kinds of pedagogical action. Pupils themselves seek details of their performance and progress. They expect written assignments to be marked and they like to know how they are getting on in their studies; assessment as 'cognitive feedback' is a basic learning condition. Few pupils, of course, take any delight in formal tests and examinations although most accept them as a normal part of schooling.

Forms of assessment are by no means new to musicians. They are well-established and accepted as part of musical life in this and many other countries. National and international competitions, which generate so much interest in musical circles and amongst a wider audience, stand out as obvious examples of activities involving 'norm-referenced' assessment procedures; participants are judged against each other. Central to the concept of assessment is the concept of objectivity; it is taken for granted, in these events, that experienced musicians can make fair and unbiased judgements about people's performances. The same principle of objectivity underpins the Grade examinations offered by the Colleges of Music. These are 'criterion referenced'; each candidate is judged against a particular standard rather than on the basis of others' achievements. Although the Grade examinations are frequently criticized, they nevertheless remain popular and attract large numbers of hopeful entrants. They are valued because they are seen as representing a particular standard of achievement which is respected throughout the world.

Pupil assessment in music, then, is a commonly accepted part of educational and musical practice, but it is an issue that has always led to differences of opinion. The National Association for Education in the Arts (NAEA) has responded positively to the principle of public assessment recognizing that such a move is 'inevitable, desirable and feasible'.[17] However, this organization quite naturally represents a variety of professional viewpoints. There are those amongst its membership who express reservations about the *value* of attempting to measure artistic achievement and development. Gillian Robinson,[18] for example, has referred to the dangers and difficulties of assessment in the context of arts education. She has also warned against adopting a single view on what is a highly complex issue; it is impossible to say that assessment is a good or bad thing until one has identified not only the techniques but also the aims of a particular strategy or proposal. These are important points; assessment is never a simple matter. Robinson is quite right to suggest that it might be all too easy to get involved in the mechanics of assessment and overlook broader aspects of the subject.

Any discussion of assessment raises a range of controversial questions such as: the relationship between assessment, teaching and learning; the performances and abilities that *can* and *should* be assessed; the techniques that might be used in schools; the ways in which assessments are used for the purpose of making decisions about individuals and groups of pupils; the connections between assessment and accountability. I shall concentrate primarily on how assessment relates to teaching and learning, although there will inevitably be some overlap with other issues.

The Task Group on Assessment and Testing (TGAT)[19] for the National Curriculum, chaired by Professor Paul Black, has from the outset directed attention to the importance of assessment in the learning process:

> Promoting children's learning is a principal aim of schools. Assessment lies at the heart of the process.[20]

The focus is on formative or on-going assessment; much emphasis is placed on the fact that information about pupils' performances enables teachers to make decisions that are vital to the planning and execution of systematic and effective pedagogy. In line with the new focus on assessment a number of teachers have reported on procedures adopted in their own schools. Michael

Taylor,[21] for example, has devised a carefully planned scheme of music profiles with the stress on the links between assessment, learning and motivation. He concludes that the results of introducing the profiles have proved to be beneficial and encouraging. Having reached a recognized standard of achievement in performing, composing and listening, pupils approach further musical studies with greater enthusiasm. But Taylor also points to the amount of time required for carrying out assessments on an *individual* basis, and this is a general problem of increased formal assessment which has been widely discussed recently in relation to Standard Assessment Tasks (SATS).

With the current emphasis on formal approaches there may be a danger of overlooking, and even inhibiting, that type of assessment which is usually described as 'informal'. This rarely receives much attention at the present time but it is central to teaching and learning. Informal assessment relates to that constant exchange of 'messages' between teachers and pupils. In musical activities teachers will be aware of the need to provide appropriate advice to pupils as they engage in creative and recreative pursuits. There is also 'self-assessment' or what learning theorists call 'intrinsic feedback'. Again, this is one of the main conditions of learning, and especially important in the learning of musical skills and techniques. Ideally, of course, all assessment in the context of learning should eventually become self-assessment; when pupils reach this stage they will have developed a state of autonomy and no longer require the services of a teacher.

Insofar as 'formal' assessment is employed for the purpose of improving teaching and learning its *aims* are unproblematic. Difficulties arise in connection with *what* can usefully be assessed, *how* it might be done and *who* should carry it out. The Exploratory Group of The Assessment of Performance Unit (APU)[22] concerned with Aesthetic Development addressed these questions and outlined a detailed model designed to measure pupils' 'knowledge of contexts', 'skill development', and ability to make appropriate 'appraisals and judgements of value'. These different components would be assessed in the context of 'forming', 'performing' and 'critical' activities. Although (for reasons unknown) the APU scheme was never implemented, many people expressed concern over the possibility of being able to measure, with any sort of accuracy, personal values and attitudes — indeed, this aspect has been ruled out by TGAT — but, of course, it might well be argued that these are the very things which should be assessed especially in arts subjects. A report indicating that pupils were highly skilful but neglecting to inform readers that the subjects actually 'hated' music would be of little use to teachers or anyone else. In fact, the APU team considered valuing to be an essential part of forming artistic appraisals. The Group also felt that 'personal preferences', although difficult to assess, should not necessarily be avoided.

Some aspects can be measured more easily than others. In musical studies assessment of individual pupil's levels of skill and information is fairly uncomplicated. Improved techniques for assessing pupils' achievements in composing, performing and listening have been developed through the GCSE initiative, but how far these can be applied more generally is uncertain because of the corporate nature of so much musical activity. Estimating a child's performance in, and contribution to, a large group activity requires very careful observations. Whether or not this can be successfully undertaken by the class teacher during normal curriculum time is very doubtful. One way of overcoming this difficulty would be to use trained observers for some aspects of the assessment. This recommendation was put forward by the APU team; it was recognized that a comprehensive scheme could not be managed by the teacher alone.

There are, of course, some major problems of assessment within the context of teaching and learning which have to be borne in mind. Many educationists have opposed formal assessments on the grounds that test results can lead to children being 'labelled'. Certainly, any data referring to pupils' performances at a particular period in their lives must be treated with circumspection. Information obtained from any *one* form of assessment can never provide a complete description of a child's capabilities; nor can it be a fully reliable indicator of future performance. Test results need to be looked at carefully and critically; this has not always been the case in practice. For example, scores obtained from standardized test batteries, designed to measure musical abilities (i.e. aptitude), tell us *something* about children's musical potential, but they never provide a full account. Unfortunately, ability test results have often been accepted far too readily; this has sometimes led to decisions being taken which were neither justified nor in the pupil's best interests. One wonders just how many children have been denied the opportunity of learning to play a musical instrument simply because they did not obtain a sufficiently high score on one of the many ability tests.

The provisional nature has also been highlighted, although in a slightly different way, by the GCSE. When the examination was first introduced some teachers expressed doubts over the possibility of objective judgements in music. But during the teacher training phases it was found that there was a surprising measure of agreement over standards; as the criteria for performing were gradually formulated this difficulty was largely (although not entirely) resolved. The same was true of the composing element. However, in an interesting research study concerned with the assessment of childrens' compositions, Desmond Sergeant and Christine Newman[23] show how there can be marked variation in judgements between different groups of assessors. Their findings seem to raise serious questions about the consistency and reliability of this aspect of the examination. This study illustrates a general limitation of assessing work, in any subject area and at any level, which goes beyond fairly basic facts and skills. However well–organized moderation procedures might be this type of summative assessment is always provisional. It is therefore mistaken to place too much reliance on the predictive uses of test and examination results.

One of the biggest criticisms and fears of formal assessment is that they inhibit the quality and range of educational encounters because of the tendency to 'teach to the tests'. Such an argument was often forwarded against the GCE examination; it was seen by some teachers as a major hindrance to curriculum development in music education. Whether or not that was ever a fully justified view is a further issue. However, a similar point is frequently made about the Grade examinations. Success in each grade becomes such a desired end that examination preparation actually restricts musical experience. For this reason the highly respected teacher and composer, Dr. Heathcote Statham, had some grave reservations about these examinations; he expressed his view in the *Musical Times* of August 1922:

> When I was a teacher at Calcutta almost every pupil I had was simply obsessed with the idea of passing a Trinity College examination. The examination became to me a sort of dreary hill of Parnassus up which I had to conduct young ladies with weariness and pain till I left them at the summit enveloped, as it were, in the full glory of the Licentiate halo. During this mountaineering feat one's eyes could scarcely ever stray from the path, one could never pause to look at the view, to envisage distant valleys, mountains or plains, because there was not time. Besides, it was not business. Business was to get to the top of the hill in the shortest possible time. Once at the summit the pupil herself became a licensed guide to the mountain, and henceforth she could conduct others up the same path. In short, examinations were an excellent stimulus to endeavour; but they took the very soul out of music.[24]

No doubt many instrumental teachers today will fully sympathize with Dr. Heathcote Statham's observations.

Although it now seems most unlikely that formal assessments in music will be as extensive as was originally envisaged, teachers will probably be required to furnish more detailed accounts of pupils' attainments. At the present time we have very limited knowledge as to what these are across the country. How *many* pupils, for example, can actually achieve the types of objectives set out in *Music from 5 to 16*?[25] For the purpose of curriculum planning any data relating to pupils' accomplishments could be informative and usable. No doubt it would have been particularly welcomed by the Subject Working Group in 1990–91 engaged in the task of devizing the new music curriculum. As we have seen, formal assessment can have a motivational and pedagogical function. But it is necessary to be alert to some of the inherent problems. For obvious reasons too much time devoted to formal assessments could very easily be detrimental to learning and development in music. More significance needs to be attached to informal assessments and the different kinds of self-assessment. Both are central to teaching and learning.

Conclusions

Many generalists in primary schools are understandably diffident about having to teach music as part of the National Curriculum. Although there are numerous schemes available to the non-specialist these can only be of use to teachers who have a sufficient understanding of the discipline, and there are no short cuts or easy ways of acquiring this understanding. Teachers who are lacking in musical confidence sometimes attempt to find a fool-proof method or scheme which appears to offer immediate solutions, but they would often be better advised to develop their own musicianship as a pre-requisite to music teaching. Let me emphasize, however, I am not suggesting that everybody who teaches music has got to be a specialist in the sense of having an advanced qualification. Some of the best music teaching I have ever seen was by a primary class teacher who was an enthusiastic, although modest, choralist. She taught her pupils to sing by singing to them, and to hear her classes perform was a great joy because the children caught her enthusiasm and love of music. Their repertoire and musical experience was limited, but I am quite sure the children were being musically educated in a thoroughly meaningful way. This teacher could not play the piano, she had never studied harmony, orchestration or history of music and she would not have called herself a musician. However, she was committed to music and understood its procedures; this is what made her such an effective practitioner.

The apparent acceptance of the objectives model as a cure-all and the possible oversimplification of sequence and progression in the new curricula are both matters which give cause for concern. There is something deceptively convincing about the hierarchical structure of subject matter as a basis for the operation of educational programmes. But where is there a school in which music or anything else is taught according to these clinical principles? Of course there is no such school. What characterizes 'good' teaching is the quality of educational experience.

The question of pupil assessment is now receiving a great deal of publicity. Although there are dangers in placing too much emphasis on formal testing all types of assessment contribute in different ways to teaching and learning. However, assessment is a complex and controversial issue with implications which go far beyond pedagogy; I shall return to these in connection with evaluation and accountability.

In the present educational climate there is much talk about the raising of standards, the achievement of learning targets and greater continuity in curricula. But improved teaching and learning are not dependent solely on more efficient planning and the realization of stated objectives. Curriculum development is built on existing practices. We need to be better informed about the nature of those practices, and information about the teaching and learning of music as a basis for curriculum development is to be obtained through the study of *classrooms*. I shall consider this further in the next chapter.

Notes and References

1 SCHAFER, R. MURRAY (1975) *The Rhinoceros in the Classroom*, Ontario, Universal Edition, p. 2.
2 GAGNE, R. (1985) *The Conditions of Learning*, (5th Ed.), New York, Holt, Reinhart and Winston.
3 TAYLOR, D. (1981) 'Towards a Theory of Musical Instruction', in PLUMMERIDGE, C. (*et al.*) *Issues in Music Education*, Bedford Way Paper No. 3, London, Kogan Page.
4 See KENDELL, I. (1976) 'If you can teach reading you can teach music', *Schools Council Dialogue*, No. 2, London, Schools Council, pp. 8–9.
5 MOORE, J. NORTHROP (Ed.) (1979) *Music and Friends. Letters to Sir Adrian Boult*, London, Hamish Hamilton (title page).
6 BOARD OF EDUCATION (1922) 'Report on Music Teaching in Secondary Schools', Circular 1252. London, Board of Education.

7   See LAWTON, D. (1983) *Curriculum Studies and Educational Planning*, London, Hodder and Stoughton, p. 17.

8   TYLER, R. (1949) *Basic Principles of Curriculum and Instruction*, Chicago, University of Chicago Press.

9   PRING, R. (1975) 'The Language of Curriculum Analysis', *The Curriculum: Studies in Education No. 2*, Institute of Education, University of London.

10 See STENHOUSE, L. (1975) *An Introduction to Curriculum Research and Development*, London, Heinemann.

11 BRUNER, J. (1963) *The Process of Education*, New York, Vintage Books, pp. 52–54.

12 MANHATTENVILLE MUSIC CURRICULUM PROGRAM (1970) *MMCP Synthesis*, New York, Media Materials Inc.

13 *Ibid.*, p. 31.

14 SWANWICK, K. and TILLMAN, J. (1986) 'The Sequence of Musical Development', *British Journal of Music Education*, *3*, 3, pp. 305–339.

15 BRUNER, J.S. (1966) *Toward a Theory of Instruction*, New York, Norton, p. 44.

16 PAYNTER, J. (1982) *Music in the Secondary School Curriculum*, Cambridge, Cambridge University Press, p. 60.

17 See SWANWICK, K. (Ed.) *Assessment in the Arts 2*, Take-Up Series, No. 8, National Association for Education in the Arts, p. 3.

18 ROBINSON, G. (1988) 'Considerations on Assessment in the Arts in the Primary Sector', SWANWICK, K. (Ed.) in *Assessment in the Arts 1*, Take-Up Series No. 7, London, National Association for Education in the Arts, pp. 39–40.

19 DEPARTMENT OF EDUCATION AND SCIENCE (1987) *National Curriculum: Task Group on Assessment and Testing: A Report*, Department of Education and Science and the Welsh Office.

20 *Ibid.*, para. 3.

21 TAYLOR, M. (1986) 'Music Profiles — A pilot Scheme', *British Journal of Music Education*, *3*, 1, pp. 19–33.

22 DEPARTMENT OF EDUCATION AND SCIENCE (1981) *Aesthetic Development. A Report from the Assessment of Performance Unit, Exploratory Group on Aesthetic Development*, Department of Education and Science.

23 SERGEANT, D. and NEWMAN, C. (1989) 'Teachers as Judges in GCSE', *Psychology of Music*, 17, p. 83.
24 Quoted in SCHOLES, P. (1947) *The Mirror of Music*, London, Novello, p. 631.
25 DEPARTMENT OF EDUCATION AND SCIENCE (1985) *Music from 5 to 16*, Curriculum Matters 4, London, HMSO, para. 25.

Chapter 5

Aspects of Evaluation

Introduction: Issues in Evaluation

Students of education often complain that evaluation is complicated and confusing. Certainly, much of the literature is highly technical and, on occasion, even esoteric. One of the main causes of confusion is that the term is used in various contexts and has therefore acquired a number of meanings; there is no single form of evaluation and, indeed, different books on the subject often appear to have little in common.[1] In a very informative survey of the field Denis Lawton[2] identifies seven 'types' of evaluation which are employed for particular purposes in education. Evaluation is concerned with the making of judgements: pedagogical, professional and political. Included amongst Lawton's types are estimations (or *assessments*) of pupil progress, teacher competence and school efficiency. These kinds of evaluation are closely related; all have become bound up with the controversial issue of accountability in education.

During the past fifteen years schools have come under much closer government scrutiny and have been required to provide more detailed information about their aims, progammes, policies and achievements. Demands for accountability reflect the view that education, rather like health care, is a public 'service'; schools have a responsibility to demonstrate that they are operating in an effective and efficient manner. The tradition of leaving education entirely to the 'professionals' is no longer acceptable for, it is said, schools have enjoyed far too much freedom. Everybody should now be entitled to enter the 'secret garden' of the curriculum.

One way in which a school may be judged efficient or 'successful' is in terms of pupils' academic attainments. It is argued by those who insist on accountabilty that the monitoring of standards and the publication of test and examination results is necessary in a democratic society. There is a large financial investment in education; tax payers have a right to know if they are getting value for money. In making decisions about their children's future education parents should be able to study different schools' academic results; this will be one important criterion by which to judge a particular school and decide on its suitability. However, the publication of results has become a contentious and highly charged issue; since there are so many variables between institutions, details of pupils' attainments can never be reliable 'performance indicators'. The point is fully appreciated by anybody who has a professional knowledge of schools and understands the most fundamental principles of educational research. However, a frequently expressed worry is that as soon as assessment data become publically available other factors tend to be ignored, especially by those who fail to recognize the intricacies of educational processes and educational institutions. These are genuine anxieties. The use of test results for the purpose of compiling 'league tables' in order to make comparisons between schools would be an invidious practice. And because of the current emphasis on accountability it is hardly surprising that many members of the teaching profession regard the move towards increased assessment with distrust and cynicism.

At the present time it seems most unlikely that judgements about a school would be based on, or even influenced by, pupils' artistic achievements as reported in tests and examinations. Nevertheless, it might be argued that since there is now so much focus on testing formal assessment in the arts is important because this will confirm their status as curriculum subjects. But whether long held assumptions which inform conceptions of the place and worth of subjects are likely to be changed by adopting this type of 'political' strategy is very doubtful. Attitudes to curriculum subjects are deep-rooted and part of a broader 'world-view' regarding what is worthwhile; they are influenced not simply by educational policies. Such attitudes reflect value positions which have become established over a very long period of time. It *may* be that the status of music and the arts would be raised if they were formally assessed along with the core subjects. Personally I am not convinced by this argument; in fact. I find it a strange and rather naive reason for advocating assessment. The status of the arts will only be enhanced by a major change in views as to what is educationally worthwhile and valuable. And this depends very largely on a greater awareness of the significance of the arts in society.

However, arts activities in the form of public events can make an important contribution to the reputation of a school. In an age of accountability and competition when schools are under greater pressure to promote their images there is always a possibility that arts activities like concerts, plays and productions may be used for merely extrinsic purposes. Such practice can have far-reaching implications for the organization and teaching of music. I shall discuss this issue further in the following chapter.

Although accountability inevitably involves some form of evaluation, information from evaluation studies will not always be used for the purpose of making judgements about an institution's *efficiency*. When new programmes, teaching strategies or materials are introduced in schools it becomes necessary to determine their suitability. What is the outcome of the innovation; is it worth pursuing further? Curriculum development is therefore dependent on evaluation. Throughout the curriculum reform era of the 1960s and 1970s a large number of national projects were introduced by agencies such as the Nuffield Foundation and the Schools Council. It was common practice to appoint an evaluator or evaluation team to monitor the effectiveness of a particular initiative. Information would then be relayed to the project team, the sponsors and other interested parties. *Curriculum* evaluation became associated not only with the estimation of pupils' performances but also with the *processes* of innovation and development.

My intention in this chapter is to concentrate on the relationship between evaluation and curriculum development.

Improvements in music education depend not on tight prescriptions or seemingly better schemes, but largely on school-based evaluation of educational programmes, a process that must be in the hands of teachers.

Curriculum Evaluation and
Curriculum Development

As the curriculum reform movement gathered momentum different project teams adopted particular styles of innovation and development; this led to the emergence of a number of evaluation models. These may be roughly categorized as either 'classical' or 'new wave' systems. Classical forms of evaluation are associated with curriculum schemes which focus on objectives; one of the most popular has been Research and Development (R and D). Ideally the development team starts by conducting research in a curriculum area in order to review current aims and practices; strengths and weaknesses are identified and taken into account when determining and recommending new courses of action. Teaching materials, incorporating appropriate objectives, are designed and then distributed to schools for implementation. The evaluator subsequently devises and administers tests, and information is sent back to the central project team. These data are then used for the purpose of further elaboration and modification of the curriculum materials.

Several Schools Council Projects started in this way but teams tended to abandon the rigidity of the model. *Music Education for Young Children*, based at the University of Reading under the direction of Arnold Bentley and later Iain Kendell,[3] was an example of an R and D approach. Clearly-defined objectives were built into highly structured materials which could be used in a variety of ways in the classroom. The evaluation of the project has not been widely publicized and to what extent it fulfilled its initial aims is unknown. In an early report there is little reference to how far pupils have achieved the stated objectives. However, there are some interesting comments about children's activities and their positive responses to the materials.[4] This shift of emphasis from objectives to activities exemplifies a typical limitation of the R and D model of evaluation. In its original form it provides little information about how the curriculum actually works when, in fact, this is just what people want to know about any curriculum initiative. The main concern tends not to be whether pupils have achieved the stated objectives. Typical questions are more likely to be: 'What is the quality of pupils' experiences? Is the project providing for more stimulating educational encounters?'

'New wave' styles of curriculum evaluation have been developed as a reaction to the limitation of classical approaches. They attempt to describe and interpret the 'realities' of classrooms rather than simply measure pupil performances. Many evaluation studies employ the same methods as those used in educational research, but whereas research findings are directed mainly towards the academic community, evaluation reports are provided for a variety of audiences and especially those in education concerned with decision making. The techniques of the new evaluators include classroom observation, interviews with teachers and often pupils, the use of questionnaires and any other methods that enable the evaluator to build up a picture of the existing curriculum. There is no *one* reality; the classroom is rich in meanings and perspectives.

The Professional Model

One of the outcomes of national development initiatives and evaluation studies was the realization that improvements in teaching and learning were not dependent simply on providing suggestions for practice together with materials for adoption and implementation in the school. In order to enhance the classroom learning environment teachers were encouraged to approach their work in a more reflective manner and engage in the processes of self-criticism and self-assessment. Their *own* evaluations of teaching and learning would generate ideas and courses of action to form the basis for curriculum development strategies. This 'professional model' of evaluation, with emphasis on the *teacher* as an evaluator, researcher and developer owes much to Lawrence Stenhouse[5] and his co-workers at the University of East Anglia. With the current policy of centralized curricula, to be evaluated largely through the testing and measurement of pupils' achievements, interest in the professional model has fallen into some decline. However, although in marked contrast to government inspired thinking on curriculum development I would argue that it offers one of the most promising and realistic ways of bringing about improvements in the teaching of music.

Stenhouse rejected the idea of curriculum development and evaluation as being two separate processes in favour of integrated classroom research. Development is seen, first and foremost, as the testing of hypotheses rather than the uncritical acceptance of prescriptive schemes or programmes of study. This does not mean that proposals for practice such as guidelines, models or teaching packs (or even the National Curriculum) originating outside the school will never be of practical value, but any proposal needs to be seen as a specification which is 'intelligent' rather than 'correct'. Teachers in schools are to be regarded as a research community, committed to the systematic study of their own practice and a willingness to share their pedagogical successes and failures.

Many of these principles are to be found in the Schools Council Project *Music in the Secondary Curriculum* directed by John Paynter.[6] The project was always teacher-focused and based on the principle that curriculum reform *starts in the classroom*.[7] Teaching materials were not produced, although in the early stages groups of teachers working in pilot schools did introduce packs of ideas for exploration in trial schools. The purpose of this exercise was to promote innovative practices which could be exchanged and shared amongst groups of teachers. During the life of the project all teachers were welcome to make their views known to the central team; this policy resulted in numerous contributions which brought together a wide range of theoretical ideals and reports of different types of practice. Ideas were disseminated through newsheets, working papers, films, tape-slide programmes and other publications. Finally, regional centres were established to enable teachers continue their professional dialogue. The object was to develop practice through an increased awareness of the significance of music as curriculum subject. Curriculum development was thus regarded essentially as *teacher* development.

A similar 'teacher oriented' approach was adopted in the *Arts and the Adolescent* project to which I have already referred in Chapter 1. The decision to establish a 'conceptual framework' (rather than produce classroom materials) was based on the view that teachers needed a theoretical language for practice. Unfortunately, for many the framework remained a fairly obscure language more suited to academic educationists. Practitioners (and more than a few theorists) found Witkin's model for arts education difficult to understand and removed from the classroom. They could not always get to grips with the principle of education as adaptation, or with the explanation of different types of knowing and creative processes. Rather than using the framework for discussion, arts teachers often spent most of their time trying to unravel its mysteries. Nevertheless, however much one may disagree with the philosophical basis of Ross and Witkin's conceptual framework, the project signalled the beginning of a new debate about arts education. Central issues were identified and dealt with in a more comprehensive and rigorous manner. Instead of recommending yet another approach to teaching Ross and Witkin asked some searching questions about the nature and purpose of arts education. Insofar as the project was intended as a means or re-awakening a more systematic interest in the arts, its aims were achieved.

This gap between academic educationists and classroom teachers is another example of the theory-practice dilemma, but since practice is informed and illuminated by a whole range of theoretical perspectives, it is necessary to find ways in which theorist and practitioners can, together, develop a meaningful and fruitful discourse. One method of achieving this would be through the establishment of what Marten Shipman has called an 'infrastructure'.[8] Shipman advocated initiatives that would 'pull together all the available services and all the current work in curriculum development'.[9] He saw teachers' centres as having an important role to play in this respect, and concluded that effective development may be largely dependent on 'narrowing the distance between schools and the agencies that administer, advise and train, or generate new ideas'.[10]

One of the conclusions of the *Arts and The Adolescent* project was that teachers of arts subjects are often isolated in schools. They have little opportunity for discussing curriculum matters pertinent to their own field. In spite of increased contacts between teachers resulting from the present educational reforms, and the creation of more arts faculties, many music teachers continue to work in situations which allow for little exchange of ideas. However, from my own experience of working with colleagues from schools on various curriculum development initiatives and INSET courses, it seems to me that most welcome and actively seek professional dialogue.[11]

What many teachers appear to find especially helpful is the opportunity of discussing everyday 'subject problems' which cannot always be shared in their own schools. These may be of a practical nature: 'How do I cope with 80 children in the hall for singing?' Sometimes problems will be more to do with attitudes towards music itself: 'The trouble is that music does not have much status in my school'. Exchange of ideas and information can reveal ways of tackling awkward practical situations since these are often common to many schools. For example, there are strategies for coping with 80 children singing in the hall which can be turned into very worthwhile experiences. We can often develop new ideas by examining aspects of teaching in discussion with colleagues. Better still, teachers will learn a great deal from visiting each other's schools in order to observe, share and reflect on different forms of organization and practice. What comes out of discussions of attitudinal problems is the importance of further publicity for music and the arts. The arts disciplines need to be brought more into the wider curriculum debate.

Exactly how far the sharing of teaching experiences does result in improved practice is never possible to estimate with any accuracy. However, many teachers express the view that exchanges help them to look more carefully at what it is they are trying to do and how they might realize their aims. Two teachers who are members of a group in a Local Education

Authority which meets regularly to study classroom practice make the following observations:

'. . . discussions have made me look more carefully at the aims of music lessons'.

'I'm much more aware of the aims, content and general planning of music lessons'.

These teachers are engaged in professional exchange about the practice they are carrying out on a daily basis. If discussion and dialogue helps practitioners to clarify the nature and purpose of their work then this is a positive step in the right direction. There is, however, evidence that there are music teachers who are still inclined to think of curriculum development in terms of new 'things to do'; development is 'taking, ideas introduced by 'expert' innovators.[12] One is forced to ask if this attitude is peculiar to the field of music education. There are numerous societies and organizations dedicated to the promotion of methodologies devised by famous educators. Perhaps it is part of the musician's way of thinking to rely on the guidance of the expert. The professional model of evaluation and development is, of course, in direct contrast to this view; the focus is on the *teacher* as both curriculum expert and developer.

Action Research

At the heart of the new professionalism is a commitment to classroom or action research, as a form of research to be carried out by teachers themselves. Curriculum development is regarded essentially as the betterment of teaching to be achieved by teachers through a more informed understanding of their own practice. The classroom is a social setting where meanings are transmitted, shared and interpreted in complex ways. In order to further understand this setting teachers are urged to study their work in a self-critical and reflective manner.

The techniques used by those who advocate action research are particularly well suited to the study and development of music teaching in schools.[13] These will include: detailed record keeping; the occasional tape recording of lessons for the purpose of critical analysis; an examination of third party observations and accounts; comments from the pupils. The use of 'triangulation' procedures which involve comparing teachers', pupils' and outside observers' perspectives has proved to be a particularly effective way of studying the multitude of factors that constitute classroom interaction. By adopting these various methods it is possible to build up a picture of the classroom reality. This, in turn, becomes the basis for making decisions about future teaching strategies. The emphasis is thus on developing *existing* practices rather than casting these aside and attempting to implement an entirely new course of action.

Two points need to be noted about this form of classroom research. First, it might be claimed that it is not research at all; its methods are too vague and lacking in objectivity and reliability. Certainly, action research is not experimental, but is in the humanistic or anthropological tradition; gathering of data relies on observations and accounts rather than the use of carefully constructed measurement instruments. And objectivity depends not on 'scientific' evidence but on teachers being able to stand back from their work and submit their findings to some form of public scrutiny. Of course, it is difficult to be self-critical and fully objective when reviewing one's own practice; the tendency is to justify action rather than criticize it.

Secondly, action research is not easy to do. The methods employed may easily lead to misunderstandings. For example, the use of observers and the adoption of triangulation procedures is likely to be seen by some as threatening. There are teachers who often feel extremely apprehensive about being observed by colleagues in the classroom. The following comments come from two experienced music teachers who had engaged in several classroom research projects:

> Not all music teachers are of the extrovert variety and while perfectly natural with a class become less so when an intruder (even a friend) is present. I don't think this is necessarily lack of professionalism but more human nature.

The personality factor must be considered — some teachers may be very intimidated by the critical presence of an observer. While accepting that evaluation is vital — I do think many teachers would feel that they'd regressed to a teaching practice situation.

One can sympathize with these teachers; it is always hard to take criticism from one's peers. But in some ways these comments might be regarded as rather surprising. After all, music teachers, possibly more than any other group, are frequently being observed by colleagues, parents, governors and inspectors during the course of school concerts and other public musical activities. Indeed, part of being a music teacher is to be a public figure. However, it may be that class music teaching and 'open' presentations, as forms of music making, are often perceived very differently. Subsequent discussions with reference to the above comments actually revealed that many teachers are particularly concerned about their lessons 'failing' because of discipline problems.

A further difficulty with action research for some teachers is the involvement of pupils. There are those express reservations and doubts about eliciting comments from pupils. I was once told by an experienced teacher that interviewing pupils is a waste of time because children cannot be trusted to tell the truth! But what is the truth; why should pupils 'make things up'? In fact pupils' comments are often very illuminating. It is how they are used that is important — like any other type of evidence pupils' views have to be treated with circumspection. Pupils' observations do not provide the basis for *immediate* action, but they are legitimate perspectives which can help to develop an understanding of teaching and learning in a school. In an extensive action research study of third year secondary pupils' attitudes, Gillian Wills[14] adopted a triangulation technique; the following extract is from an interview conducted by a third party.

Interviewer: What activities do you do in music?
Pupil 1:   . . . it's the same every week.
Pupil 2:   No, it's not.

Pupil 3:	It is not.
Pupil 1:	It is ...
Pupil 4:	No, it's not really ...
Pupil 1:	We have to do ... we're given out instruments and we've got the notes and everyone just plays what they do and then at the end of the lesson we all play it together.
Pupil 2:	She ... we ... we don't 'cos sometimes we have to ... say she puts a record on we do things to that ... But sometimes we play instruments together in a class to a tune like a pop tune ... sometimes that comes out quite good ... Sometimes, we do written music ... its all different ... its not the same.
Pupil 1:	Yeah, and in the second year we just used to play music, we just used to tap the things ... it was anything ... but now with ... we're supposed to know how to read music and everything and we didn't do that in the first and second years ...
Pupil 4:	No, it's not that ... it's the teacher ...
Pupil 2:	We've always had different teachers ...
Pupil 1:	I think ... I think we should have been taught how to read music in the first year soon as we started to do it ...
Pupil 4:	But in the first year we used to do silly things, play music ... bang bang on the xylophones ...
Pupil 3:	We still do the same things ...
Pupil 1:	Play a tambourine ...
Pupil 4:	But we know a bit more ...
Interviewer:	So you think that shaking tambourines and playing xylophones was silly and that it wasn't teaching you anything ... Is that right?
Pupil 2:	Well, we did that in primary school anyway.

Pupil 3:	We're not learning anything.
Pupil 1:	Just banging a tambourine . . . just doing nothing, really it wasn't worth it.
Pupil 4:	Yeah, because we used to have this teacher . . . but she's left now and we used to all kind of like . . . bang bang on the table . . .
Pupil 1:	Bang bang bop beat stop.
Pupil 4:	It was . . . nothing.
Pupil 1:	It used to be rubbish . . .

Personally, I find these comments to be very revealing. There are some clear messages about teaching, learning, continuity, progression and general provision for music. Of course, this sort of data cannot be used for making generalizations about music education. But together with other types of evidence the observations do provide some information about *that* class in *that* school. Future pedagogical action will not be determined solely by such information, but to ignore it would obviously be shortsighted.

In another investigation concerned with attitudes Kathryn Hill[15] set out to examine secondary school pupils' memories of their music experiences in the primary school.

Interviewer:	What did you enjoy most about all this music? In your school — what was the best thing do you think?
Pupil:	Well, I just liked it 'cos it was nice. I just liked playing the recorder. I like wood instruments, and . . . it was fun. We used to play funny things as well.
Interviewer:	And you liked that. What did you enjoy least?
Pupil:	I didn't really like it when we used to do difficult — he used to just suddenly put our music on the board and we didn't know how to play it, and we'd have to pretend to play because if you didn't play it, he'd, you know, shout at you. He

	thinks you know how to read the music, but you don't. We told him that we don't know, but he just says we do.
Interviewer:	So you had to mime?
Pupil:	Yes.

This is a good example of 'alternative realities'. It is most unlikely that the teacher would have shared the pupil's view of what was happening in the music lesson! Again, the pupil's comments should not be regarded as the one true account of the episode, but they do provide evidence which sheds light on the nature of an educational encounter.

In order to overcome the threatening aspects of action research teachers are encouraged to work with others who are committed to the same ideals. This is the principle of the research community. For the music teacher in isolation there are obviously limitations as to how far this type of research can be carried out. Action research has not been employed in music education to the same extent as in other curriculum areas such as Science and Humanities. Nevertheless, in some Local Authorities groups of music teachers are working together along these lines. My own view is that such exercises are likely to be more productive than the writing of guidelines. A guideline might be useful in offering some sense of direction, but it can only deal in generalities. Action research is concerned with the reality of practice. Findings contribute to the making of decisions about how it could or should be. This takes us back to the question: 'What are we looking for in our own music teaching?' Here is where an underlying theory of musical experience and understanding becomes the basis for critical reflection. *This is music education in theory and practice*. The theory becomes more of a reference point than a guide.

Of course, an action research approach to curriculum development is very demanding in terms of time and staffing. With issues like appraisal and accountability uppermost in people's minds, notions of failures as well as successes might militate against what Stenhouse called an 'open and honest' approach to teaching. 'Success' is the order of the day and to admit to failure may be to take a dangerous professional step.

But in an important sense that is what it is to be a professional educationist. This is a factor that many people, and particularly politicians, fail to understand. There is now so much political comment about education that some people are coming to believe that children are sitting in classrooms simply waiting to be taught by 'good' teachers. But educational practice is never like this. The curriculum is an immensely complex process, and its improvement depends, in part, on careful and systematic study carried out against the background of properly formulated principles. Of course, curriculum development plans based on action research and professional dialogue will not transform the field of music education overnight. But then there are no simple formulas for success in teaching and learning.

Conclusion

There is much talk these days of the need to raise standards in education and for schools to be accountable to the society they serve. Those who beat the standards drum with monotonous regularity often give the impression that teachers have become complacent about pupils' achievements. This is quite untrue. Professional educators are always striving towards improving the effectiveness and quality of their work in schools. Education is a value-laden enterprise; the notion of improvement is built into it. Working towards better practice is an intrinsic educational aim and part of what it is to be an educator.

I have advocated an approach to curriculum development in music education which arises out of the professional model of evaluation and development. It is an approach which brings together theoretical perspectives and classroom practices. The types of questions that music teachers will ask of their practices will be: Are these pupils being initiated into the aesthetic field of music through this activity? Do they demonstrate a growing understanding of musical procedures? Are we establishing a musical environment in this school? The answers to these questions will be obtained through the use of different techniques: formal and informal assessments; pupils' comments; detailed records of lessons; critical reflections; third-party observations.

Curriculum development is a continuous process of action and reaction.

There are, however, traditions, attitudes, practices and policies that contrast sharply with the professional model. The setting up of infrastructures, classroom research strategies and curriculum discussion groups are all time consuming and demanding on teachers' energies. With new forms of administration and management teachers are likely to find it increasingly difficult to visit each other's schools. Curriculum development based on the principles of the professional model does not offer immediate solutions. But that is its strength; curriculum development is always a slow and evolutionary process. Changes in the quality of practice do not occur quickly; they are piecemeal, hesitant and uneasy. They are no panaceas in curriculum reform. To some extent the professional model may be regarded as inappropriate in the present educational climate. The current emphasis is on rational planning as a basis for 'success'. I would argue strongly against this 'industrial' and mechanistic view of the curriculum. All educational practice is a mixture of successes and failures, and an understanding of failures is just as important in development strategies as is the identification and dissemination of success.

In this and the previous two chapters I have been discussing music mainly as a curriculum subject. However, as I stated at the beginning of the book musical activities beyond the classroom must also be regarded as part of the field of music education. In the following chapter I shall consider music in the wider context of the school and the community.

Notes and References

1 Compare, for example, COLWELL, R. (1970) *The Evaluation of Music Teaching and Learning*, Englewood Cliffs, New Jersey, Prentice Hall, with TAWNEY, D. (Ed.) (1976) *Curriculum Evaluation Today: Trends and Implications*, London, MacMillan.

2 LAWTON, D. (1983) *Curriculum Studies and Educational Planning*, London, Hodder and Stoughton, (Chapter 7).

3 KENDELL, I. (1976) *Time for Music. Teachers Support Book*, London, Arnold.

4 FAWCETT, B. (1981) *The Gloucester Evaluation of Time for For Music*, University of Reading School of Education.

5 STENHOUSE, L. (1975) *An Introduction to Curriculum Research and Development*, London, Heinemann.

6 PAYNTER, J. (1982) *Music in the Secondary School Curriculum*, Cambridge, Cambridge University Press.

7 SCHOOLS COUNCIL (1974) *Music in the Secondary Curriculum*, News Sheet One, London, Schools Council.

8 SHIPMAN, M. (1974) *Inside a Curriculum Project*, London, Methuen.

9 *Ibid.*, p. 174.

10 *Ibid.*, p. 174.

11 Teachers' comments in this and the following section are taken, unless otherwise stated, from my own small-scale evaluations of INSET courses and curriculum development projects in Local Education Authorities.

12 Many teachers have expressed this view. See also PAYNTER (1982), *op. cit.*, p. 18.

13 A good introduction to these techniques is to be found in NIXON, J. (Ed.) (1981) *A Teacher's Guide to Action Research*, London, Grant McIntyre.

14 WILLS, G. (1980) *An Investigation into the Interests and Attitudes of Secondary School Children Towards Music: A Case Study*, Unpublished M.A. Dissertation, Institute of Education, University of London.

15 HILL, K. (1983) *The Secondary School Intake and the Music Curriculum*, Unpublished M.A. Dissertation, Institute of Education, University of London.

Chapter 6

Music in School and Community

Introduction

My aim in this chapter is to examine the scope of music in schools and consider how different factors — aesthetic, social, pedagogical, professional, political — contribute to the shaping of music education systems and practices. Our present system may be seen as a fusion of the elementary and independent school traditions of class teaching and voluntary musical activities. It is, therefore, not hard to understand why there are people, even within education, who have an impression of music in schools as being concerned largely with the promotion of choirs, orchestras, jazz bands, recorder consorts and other ensembles. These groups seldom rehearse during normal curriculum time, but it is they who represent the field of music education on public occasions. Over the past fifty years there has been a steady growth of extracurricular activities in maintained schools. Standards of performance have gradually risen and the high achievements of young musicians are acknowledged through national events like the School Proms. Whilst these developments are to be applauded it can sometimes happen that over-concentration on extracurricular pursuits inadvertently leads to a neglect of regular curriculum programmes. This will obviously be to the disadvantage of those pupils — often the majority — who experience music only through general class lessons. However, the reasons for undue attention to the extra-curricula activities are not always easily explained. Areas of the curriculum are social as well as intellectual or pedagogical systems; different forces determine their mode of operation.

Concerts, plays, productions and other artistic events, usually prepared during out-of-school hours, have always been valued for their contribution to the general style and ethos of the educational institution. These celebrations bring with them the magic of the arts for all to share; they permeate and animate the life of a school in a very special and powerful way. Arts presentations are particularly appreciated by parents and members of the local community. Indeed, without such activities schools would be very different and almost certainly poorer places.

Music in schools encompasses a wide range of pursuits and it is apparent that teachers are required to be versatile and flexible musicians. They are expected to organize and direct musical activities in a variety of settings; consequently they assume the role of general practitioners. Like all teachers, music specialists face new challenges in an evolving educational system. Their additional duties, responsibilities and commitments will inevitably have an impact on the development of the music curriculum. And as the role of the music teacher changes it becomes necessary to review patterns of teacher education and training.

Curriculum and Extracurriculum

The music teacher's dual role of classroom practitioner and musical director is familiar to everybody working in music education. It is usually more evident in the secondary school; but it is also common practice for primary specialists (consultants or coordinators) to organize extra musical activities as well as take overall responsibility for the normal programme of class lessons. In some cases, particularly at secondary level, it might even seem as if music teachers devote most of their time and energy to the extracurricular dimension. There tends to be an assumption in many schools that teachers of music will arrange various musical activities and mount concerts and other events. Consequently, teachers have the task of trying to implement and develop the music curriculum and at the same time maintain a range of other non-timetabled pursuits; this can often lead to problems of management and organization. However, the practice of music education is also determined by social and political factors that are rapidly exerting a stronger influence in the new educational climate.

It is very doubtful whether music teachers are under any *legal* obligation to take on these extra duties. Nevertheless, failure to do so can result in their losing credibility in the eyes of those to whom they feel morally and professionally accountable.[1] Understandably, teachers wish to demonstrate to the Head, colleagues, parents and governors that they are carrying out their duties effectively; and it is, of course, through the extracurricular dimension of their work that they are most likely to gain recognition and approval. A teacher of music might be known within a small circle of interested parties as a good classroom practitioner or an imaginative innovator, but his chances of promotion and increased status in the school are often much more likely to be gained as a result of a public image. In an interesting sociological analysis of teaching, focusing on status and role, Cannon has suggested that:

> Within an occupation as stratified as teaching, the one with the higher prestige is the teacher whose role is most akin to that of a university lecturer ... the sixth-form teacher.[2]

In a similar way, it can be argued that the music teacher will acquire higher status if he is regarded by school colleagues more as a professional musician, and one way in which he can achieve this status is through conducting concert performances of the school orchestra or choir. If it does happen that teachers place particular emphasis on the development of extracurricular activities and public performances in order to improve their own standing, then justification for these pursuits is difficult to uphold. In fact, from this perspective extracurricular activities could easily be regarded as essentially anti-educational; they might well be seen as being in the interests of teachers rather than pupils.

Now let me say, unequivocally, lest my remarks be misunderstood, I am not suggesting that hard-working and dedicated teachers are consciously manipulating and exploiting pupils to some dubious and sinister end. As musicians, teachers value choirs, orchestras and ensembles; they know from their own experience the joy and satisfaction of corporate music making. They quite rightly feel it is part of their professional duty to ensure that their pupils have every opportunity of participating in these musical activities. But it is also necessary to recognize that within the social system of a school there are underlying messages that can, and do, have a direct effect on daily practices and attitudes towards areas of the curriculum. It is possible that class music programmes will be neglected when teachers feel obliged to concentrate on extracurricular activities and preparations for concerts because this is their perception of what is required of them. And in schools where great importance is attached to public presentations the message may be quite explicit. In these circumstances music teachers can be forced into an unenviable position.

I was recently asked to assist at a school concert; this was to be a special event, so I was informed, and part of a broader strategy aimed at publicizing the school within the local community. It is well-known that because of new funding arrangements, schools find themselves in the strange and unprecedented situation of competing with each other. Staff feel the need to convince parents of prospective pupils that their school is as good as, or better than, another in the locality. Concerts and other artistic enterprises can become effective promotional exercises. We hear stories of Heads using music for the purpose of window-dressing and public relations. I have no idea just how widespread this might be although I suspect many teachers will be well aware of such practices. Of course, it is important not to be self-righteous over this issue. Schools are naturally and understandably proud of their musical traditions and achievements. There is certainly nothing objectionable about a public exhibition of artistic activities.

But it would be a scandal if the arts came to be regarded as purely commercial products and valuable only insofar as they could be used for advertising and attracting customers. Apart from the ethical conflicts which arise from these policies the educational outcomes could be quite disastrous. One might imagine a situation in which certain traditions, repertoires, innovations and experiments were avoided for fear of giving the school the wrong type of reputation. This would hardly be conducive to the development of a dynamic form of music *education.*

It may begin to seem as if my remarks are a typical example of what sociologists call the 'making' of problems, derived from a neo-Marxist interpretation of educational institutions, namely, that schools are conspiratorial places that actually work against education and the interests of pupils. I do not subscribe to such a view but there is a dilemma over the relationship between curriculum and extracurricular activities; it needs to be faced and brought out into the open. The form of music education I have been proposing throughout this book is one that enables *all* children to extend their musical potential through imaginative encounter and exposure to many different styles, traditions and genres. It is dependent on appropriate and supportive attitudes, suitable organizational structures and proper staffing levels. While teachers feel compelled to present music for public consumption in order to boost the reputation of the school, curriculum programmes will suffer neglect. There is a serious danger of the arts becoming showpieces in a competitive education system increasingly subject to market forces. Throughout history, music and the arts have been used for extrinsic ends and this has frequently led to their being distorted and devalued. If this is allowed to happen in schools, arts *educators* will feel a loss of integrity. There is the possibility of a strong reaction *against* extracurricular activities if teachers and pupils believe that arts events are appreciated simply for their commercial usefulness. This would be extremely regrettable since there are good *educational* reasons why these activities should be supported and encouraged.

Musical, Personal, Social and Community Education

Participation in a school concert or musical production, even though it may be at a very modest level, provides for a particular type of musical experience; it is one that is rather different from what is normally possible in the class lesson. In many cases what is sung or played in a concert is learned and rehearsed as part of the timetabled curriculum programme. But a performance to an audience has the effect of sharpening an awareness of musical procedures. All musicians are conscious of the pressures and demands of the concert performance: the need for extra concentration; the desire to give one's best; the ability to keep going when there are technical slips. These dispositions are vital in music making; their development is an essential part of becoming musically intelligent. Consequently, there is a valid argument in favour of all children having *more* opportunities to take part in concerts and other musical events during their school years. In a detailed study of extracurricular activities, Tee Sook Leng[3] asked pupils about their views on school concerts:

Interviewer: Do you get anything out of it (a concert performance)?

Pupil A: Oh yeah, you always get something out of the occasion, don't you?

Interviewer: What do *you* get out of it?

Pupil A: It's just more exciting than a rehearsal, isn't it — you know — get the adrenalin flowing a bit more — you know — get more worked up, I suppose.

Pupil D: I like the excitement of the concerts — all those people watching you — you just can't make a mistake.

Pupil G: The actual concerts, I think I like them best 'cos I like the whole atmosphere, the excitement and things. That's the best part of it.

One of the most valuable outcomes of participating in public events is that musical and social experiences are combined in a special way for pupils. Anybody who actually teaches music in school and organizes concerts and productions will be aware of the keen sense of artistic excitement and social cohesion that is generated on these occasions. Pupils of different ages, abilities and backgrounds are working together in a cooperative manner and sharing a common commitment to the success of the venture. This involves individuals being conscious of their responsibility within a team and recognizing and respecting the contribution of others. The educational value of such experience has been strongly commended by David Hargreaves,[4] who argues that through arts activities children acquire a sense of solidarity and personal dignity. This is seen by Hargreaves as being in contrast to the tradition of schooling which focuses on *individual* success. He maintains that emphasis on the individual frequently leads to a sense of failure on the part of the many, and that this is one of the main causes of educational alienation. Using the performance of a school play as an example, Hargreaves suggests:

> Individual performers may be outstanding and get credit for it. But the success of the few does not, as happens in classrooms, automatically generate a sense of failure in the rest. Those with more lowly contributions know perfectly well that they could not be the 'star' of the show, but they know that they have been making a contribution which is essential to the whole enterprise and which is thus known to be valued. A play thus gives the participants dignity.... Each makes a contribution, the competent execution of which brings a sense of being valued. Solidarity and dignity are conferred simultaneously.[5]

Cooperative arts projects provide unique opportunities for children to develop 'as persons'. I am quite sure that many music teachers would agree with Hargreaves and be able to give examples of how individual children have developed in confidence and self-esteem through involvement in corporate musical making. There are children who seem to do remarkably well in choirs, orchestras, bands and musical productions, but are otherwise regarded not necessarily as failures but certainly not as high achievers. By providing for and releasing artistic capacities their talents, or intelligences, become recognized. I am always particularly impressed by the musical and artistic achievements of many pupils in special schools. One often wonders why these children, so many of whom are understandably lacking in confidence through a sense of educational failure, are not given far greater opportunity to engage in arts projects. This is not to suggest that music and the arts are especially suited to the education of the so-called less able. Personal and social education is of the greatest importance for all pupils, and the arts have a very significant function in this respect.

Musical events will be of educational value not only to those who are directly involved in the performing. Many pupils are likely to have ancillary duties; it is necessary that they too should be made to feel part of the team. In fact, artistic activities can add something to everybody's lives and become focal points for contacts between pupils, teachers, parents and members of the local community. It is not unusual for parents to learn far more about their children's school through attending a concert or production rather than from formal meetings with teachers. There is an important sense in which the values of the school are embodied in these artistic presentations, not merely in the performances, but in their total organization.

A very positive educational trend in recent years has been the establishment of closer contacts between schools and the local community through arts ventures. These moves are providing further opportunities for personal and social education (PSE). However, rather than viewing community activities as occasions when music can be used *for* PSE it would be preferable to think of them as ways of *uniting* different forms of education. One of the aims of the *Music Performance and Communication Skills Project*,[6] introduced at the Guildhall School of Music and Drama, is to assist performance students in developing a broader musical outlook; this is to be achieved partly through engagement in activities which take place in a wide variety of social contexts. The Director of the project, Professor Peter Renshaw, holds the view that the arts can make a meaningful contribution not only to the development of individuals but also to the betterment of society. He maintains this is dependent on musicians acquiring a range of social skills which will enable them to share their music in different community venues. But this project does not simply provide opportunities for students to perform in alternative settings such as prisons, hospices or community centres; it involves a fundamental reappraisal of artists and arts in society. Renshaw is concerned with breaking down those barriers which isolate musicians and perpetuate the 'star' image of the performer. It is this isolation of music and musicians, the distancing of performers from audiences, which permeates thinking about musical activity and creates the impression of music as an exclusive discipline.

Although the project is based in a specialist music college, and designed for advanced musicians, its basic philosophy has implications for the development of attitudes and practices in schools. One of the main criticisms of extracurricular activities has been that they foster an 'elitist' conception of music. Certainly, musical exclusiveness can be engendered if small performing groups are placed on a pedestal and regarded as the school's chief musical representatives. This does sometimes occur because the star image, which Renshaw is so anxious to expunge, has a strongly pervasive effect on our thinking about musical performance. There is a view that public musical occasions should be limited to a display of the highest standards by the best performers; this attitude may be seen as a reflection of the western concert hall ideal.[7] When music does become exclusive in schools the majority of children may well be inclined to regard it as the preserve of the talented or gifted; music is *not* for everybody. It is this perception of music that has so often been detrimental to the development of music education. But performing activities do not have to be confined to only the most able; in many schools large numbers of pupils of all abilities are involved in a range of musical presentations. And to adopt this policy is in no way to imply that performing groups should aim at anything other than the highest possible standards.

The Guildhall project also suggests ways of organizing activities. There are numerous examples of teachers forging links with the local community, leading to music becoming an important form of community experience and community service. I have a report from a teacher in a primary school describing contacts made through music between her pupils and members of a Senior Citizens Club. The children regularly visit the club and present short concerts; apparently these are always received with much appreciation and enthusiasm. The teacher comments:

> Of course, the highlight for the children is the tea and cakes supplied afterwards when they mingle with the old people. Both parties thoroughly enjoy themselves.

The observation should not be treated lightly. Those of us who participate in similar activities know that this type of small concert can be of enormous significance in the lives of those involved. The educational outcome of these experiences cannot be quantified or easily expressed in words, yet teachers who arrange similar local events will acknowledge their value. They provide for one of the most meaningful forms of personal and social education, bringing people together in a way which fosters community understanding, social sharing and a sense of unity.

At a secondary school, with which I have been associated for many years, the music staff decided to form a choir to enable pupils, staff, parents and indeed anybody interested in singing, to join together in music making. Like so many school projects this one has never been properly evaluated; my limited observations are based on semi-structured interviews with the teachers and written comments from parents and pupils. Practices were held during the evenings on a weekly basis. The choir became very much a feature of the school with a special relationship developing between members of very different groups. Musical activity became a strong binding force for the participants. From the point of view of music education the choir provided for a type of musical experience which would otherwise not have been available to pupils. Because it was based in the school pupils felt confident about attending rehearsals; singing in the local choral society would probably have never crossed their minds. Similarly, several parents openly admitted to having wanted to sing in a choir for many years. Previously they had lacked the courage to inquire about joining an established music society; they felt much more at home in their children's school. Many members of the choir valued the social contacts and new friendships. The music staff, however, were always anxious to emphasize that the choir was essentially a musical and educational enterprise. The experience of community arose naturally out of the musical activity.

These two brief examples of links between schools and the local community are in no way exceptional. There are many instances where schools are reaching out through musical and other forms of artistic activity. Although I have been stressing music education as part of personal and social education I do not wish to imply that I am advocating the arts on purely social grounds. However, I would maintain that the social dimension of music is of importance; it is often not sufficiently recognized in the context of music education.

Providing opportunities for pupils, parents, members of staff and the local community to participate together in music is one of the best ways of raising greater awareness of the arts and the value of arts education. However, there are some attitudes which actually lead to a resistance to these sorts of initiatives. One hears it said, for example, that to have parents, peripatetic staff and other guests playing in the school orchestra is in a sense cheating because subsequent performances are not actually a true indicator of pupils' work. But what is the *purpose* of a school orchestra? It provides for a particular type of musical and educational experience, and if this can be improved and extended through the assistance of staff and parents then their involvement is to be welcomed. Those who oppose this type of cooperative venture often hold the competitive view of education and music education. Extracurricular activities are seen as a measure of the school's achievements, and to bolster a concert by drawing on the assistance of outsiders is seen as not playing the game. As I have already suggested, changes in the educational system may have contributed to a hardening of this attitude and overshadowed the true value of corporate artistic activity.

There can, of course, be many occasions when parents and members of the community can join pupils in music events. The establishment of wider links can also be highly beneficial in terms of the curriculum. There will be various human resources — individuals and groups — who can make a contribution to the development of arts curricula, and it may be that these external resources are not always recognized and employed as they could be. More consultation and cooperation with arts organizations beyond the school will be another way of bringing people's attention to arts education and to the opportunities the arts offer for creating a sense of community. School-based community arts festivals and projects would seem to be ideally suited to the furthering of the arts both in schools and society.

The Teacher's Task

Music in school includes an increasing number of activities, and teachers have to respond to many different musical demands. They are expected to be all-round musicians who have a range of skills, a broad expertise and a certain type of approach to music-making. One of the most appropriate models for the teacher is the eighteenth century Kappelmeister. To adopt this model is *not* to emphasize the Director of Music function. The Kappelmeister was very much a generalist musician; even the most famous often had a variety of duties that can be compared with those of the present day school music specialist.[8] Of course, comparisons should not be taken too far, and clearly there are significant differences between the two roles. But they both represent a style of musicianship which is characterized by its versatility and an ability to adapt and modify practices when circumstances demand. It is an approach to musical activity markedly different from that of the specialist performer; it is one that requires a certain type of *creative* orientation. Although music educators have shown a wide interest in creativity in recent years much of this interest has centred on the process of composition and how children might develop their creative abilities. Relatively little thought has been given to the idea of music teaching itself as being a creative enterprise. We talk about the skilful teacher when referring to a practitioner who has rather special pedagogical accomplishments. But to what extent is it possible to regard teaching not only as skilful but also creative?

Psychological explanations of creativity, as described by theorists such as Koestler[9] and Guilford,[10] focus on creativity as a cognitive style involving: imaginative thinking; making leaps, transforming ideas, spotting alternatives; solving problems in a novel way. Creativity in this operational sense can be applied to almost any aspect of musical behaviour. Arranging music is an interesting example. The much-admired carol arrangements of Willcocks and Rutter, charming works like Kodaly's *Matra Pictures* or Vaughan William's *Folk Songs from Somerset*, are all illustrations of how relatively simple materials have been *transformed* into new musical structures. Composing and arranging for unusual instrumental ensembles or for groups of performers with widely differing skills and experiences are further instances of the ability to see musical possibilities and alternatives. In fact composers frequently demonstrate this type of thinking. The young Haydn at Eisenstadt was faced with the problem of having two outstanding players in his orchestra, namely the violinst Tomasini and the cellist Weigl. In his Symphony No. 6 (Le Matin) we find special parts for these two exceptional players. Haydn's creativity is exemplified in this instance, not only in the *musical value* of his composition but also in the musical embodiment of the solution to what was the practical problem of how to use the talents of the more accomplished instrumentalists in a 'mixed-achievement' orchestra.

These examples of a particular aspect of musical creativity as exhibited in the work of composers may seem rather removed from the routine practice of music education, but they do suggest *approaches* to music teaching. There will be many instances when the teacher, like the composer, will be confronted with musical problems which require musical solutions: organizing activities for children with varying levels of skill and technique; arranging music for unlikely combinations of instruments; preparing materials for different types of projects. Central to the task of teaching is the intention to bring about learning. However, *educating* goes far beyond simply meeting this necessary condition. Education in music involves initiating pupils into the procedures of the discipline; it involves introducing children to the mystery, magic and delight of musical experience. The teacher is required to *transform* inert materials and prescribed outlines into vital and dynamic encounters. And it is this process of transformation that bears the mark of the creative act. It involves a combination of musical insight and those pedagogical skills of presentation, organization and communication. Creative teaching is an attitude towards practice; the creative teacher is the person who can make connections between the worlds of music and music education. In fact, solutions to many of the problems of music education are to be found in *music itself*. And the ability of teachers to see these connections and work in a creative manner will obviously be dependent, to some extent, on their education and training. I shall consider this issue further in the following section.

Teachers of music in schools assume a growing number of pedagogical, administrative and managerial duties and responsibilities. As the role of the music teacher changes so do priorities. Traditionally, many music specialists have devoted time to the maintenance and development of their own musicianship through being involved in musical activities beyond the school. This has always been regarded as important and necessary; participation in musical pursuits informs teaching. Some teachers are not unnaturally concerned that with ever increasing demands their personal musicianship may well suffer. They feel the need to be practising musicians, but increase in administrative tasks may have the effect of eroding their creativity.

For many teachers their job specification appears to be quite unreasonable; this has been recognized for some years. In 1962, John Horton, Her Majesty's Staff Inspector for Music, observed that:

> State schools ... have grafted on to the State system of class teaching as much of the public school tradition as they can, assemblies with quite elaborate music, choirs, madrigials, orchestras, bands and music clubs. Nobody is noticing that you have got, not merely somebody taking classes in music but somebody who is also acting as Director of Music, and you have got to try to combine the two traditions on one kind of staffing. I think we shall have on look very, very closely at this and watch the strain on our teachers, because we are doing so much with so many fine teachers that I think we are imposing a very heavy strain on some of the best of them through

their very success, and through the fact that they are making the best of both these worlds.[11]

The situation has not changed. One is bound to ask if the present scope of school music is essentially impractical. Certainly, there are music teachers who find themselves in the position of having to carry an unrealistic workload. They often spend long periods of non-directed time (far more than is generally realized) rehearsing groups in preparation for concerts and other school functions. In large schools, where there are two or three full-time music staff, this work can be evenly distributed. But there are many secondary schools in which one teacher has the sole responsibility for the whole programme of musical activities. In some cases, visiting instrumental teachers will assist with bands and orchestras. However, with the reduction and withdrawal of instrumental services there is every likelihood that such arrangements will become less commonplace.

Although I have emphasized the value of music in the school and the wider community I take it as axiomatic that music education is first and foremost music in the classroom, available to *all* children as part of a liberal education. This has been the consistent message from music educators over many years and it is a central theme in this book and the series to which it belongs. If music is to be taught effectively within the curriculum it may be necessary to 'rationalize' extracurricular programmes. Nevertheless, the influence of accountability can impinge on a classroom-based concept of music education in a number of different ways. I have already referred to the present competitive atmosphere within education and the desire to demonstrate efficiency; both of these factors can lead to concentration on the extracurricular with subsequent negative effects on the development of music as a curriculum subject.

However, with the introduction of teacher appraisal the situation could well change. Inevitably, more attention will be given to class programmes; this could be a fruitful development. But current proposals for appraisal are highly problematic. They rest on the assumption that it is possible to identify good practice, and they are also associated with the need to confront weak practice and take appropriate action. The intriguing questions about appraisal are: By what criteria does one classify the 'good' or 'bad' teacher? Who should carry out the appraisal?

As I have already suggested, when discussing the issue of objectives and processes in Chapter 4, we can recognize good practice. However, judgements can never be based entirely on pedagogical strategies, such as classroom organization, teacher-pupil relationships and communication; teaching strategy cannot be separated from the content of lessons and the curriculum programme as a whole. Many adverse judgements about teaching are more to do with *what* is being taught rather than the technical efficiency of the teacher, but this aspect may be simplified as a result of greater central control over the content of the curriculum. While teacher appraisal might lead to greater focus on music in the classroom, it could also restrict and stifle curriculum development, because teachers may become concerned over choosing the 'wong' activities and materials. Like so many of the current educational reforms the principles, details and further implications of teacher appraisal have hardly been considered.

Teacher appraisal is also associated with what Denis Lawton has called 'bureaucratic' (as opposed to 'democratic') accountability.[12] The bureaucratic model of 'line management' suggests a hierarchical structure in which the teacher is accountable to the Head, who in turn is accountable to the School Governors and the Local Education Authority. Democratic accountability, on the other hand, leads to a network in which all parties in the education system recognize their responsibilities to each other. Accounts are shared and negotiated amongst professionals in a positive manner for the purpose of bringing about improvements. This is very much in keeping with the professional model of evaluation and development which I have proposed (in Chapter 5) as the most effective approach to the development of the music curriculum. However, all the signs are that we are moving more towards a bureaucratic style of accountability and therefore towards closed and guarded forms of communication. Such an environment would be the very antithesis of one that supported open and honest exchanges and the sharing of pedagogical successes and failures.

Increasing demands for accountability present a number of

distinct problems for the future of music education. If schools feel the need to be accountable to society in the sense of projecting a 'good image' the tendency will be to emphasize the achievements of pupils in extracurricular activities. The newly proposed scheme of teacher appraisal with its bureaucratic associations does not augur well for a form of curriculum development in music education based on the principle of the teacher as a reseacher within a research community. However, accountability exercises will undoubtedly draw attention to what is going on in schools. More public knowledge of the field of arts education could help to enhance the status of the arts subjects; it could also ensure their future as important disciplines within a broad and balanced education.

Teacher Education

Any consideration of the role of music teachers inevitably raises questions about their professional education and training. This is a subject that is now being widely discussed by educationists, politicians and members of the public. One only has to scan the pages of the *Times Educational Supplement* or the *Education Guardian* to appreciate that opinion is sharply divided over existing patterns of initial training. Almost every week some distinguished educationist outlines a proposal for modifications and reforms. I do not intend to profer yet another grand scheme; I shall confine my remarks to some comments that relate to the topics so far discussed in this chapter.

In the report of *Music in the Secondary School Curriculum*[13] the point is made that training institutions place too much emphasis on students acquiring traditional forms of musical expertise, including high standards in individual instrumental performance, conducting skills and academic knowledge. Whilst these capabilities are recognized as obviously valuable and important, it is argued that teachers in training also require more opportunities to compose and arrange music for themselves; they need to explore the medium in ways which will lead to a greater musical insight. What is really being called into question is not only the professional inappropriateness of some present forms of musical training but also the idea of the accomplished performer or the academic musician as representing paradigms of musical achievement. Such musicians are likely to hold attitudes towards music which can be incompatible with those of the school music teacher, who is the 'all-rounder' or what I have called the creative general practitioner.

In the current debate little thought appears to be given to how patterns of initial teacher education might be determined by the nature of teaching in particular subject areas. Education and training courses for mathematics teachers are not necessarily suitable for music teachers. For example, one of the shortcomings of the 'consecutive' mode of training is that musicians with relatively specialist backgrounds of university or conservatoire studies have to acquire not only a range of generalist competencies but also a wider view of music in a very short period of time. An advantage of a 'concurrent' course is that it can provide a better opportunity for educating and training the musician who needs a broader expertise. This policy has been adopted in a number of countries.[14] It is based on the view that the school music teacher requires a particular form of musicianship training; to attempt this in one postgraduate year is not feasible.

But whether or not it is any longer sufficient for the music teacher to be simply a particular type of musician is debatable. With the increase of faculty structures in schools teachers will require skills and understanding *across* the arts. This is likely to mean that the content of courses will have to be substantially reviewed and modified. If music teachers are to work effectively in combined arts departments it will be necessary to introduce forms of training and education for music specialists which include more studies in the other arts disciplines. Again the question arises as to how far the consecutive mode is entirely suited to the changes taking place in the philosophy and practice of arts education.

In Chapter 4 I referred to the difficulties encountered by general class teachers in primary schools who are required to teach music but are themselves lacking in musical skill, experience and confidence. An inquiry into the position of the arts in the initial training of primary teachers was carried out in 1985 by Shirley Cleave and Caroline Sharpe.[15] This was prompted by earlier research findings indicating that in many schools provision for arts education left much to be desired. Cleave and Sharpe's comprehensive and highly informative report shows that whilst some 75% of primary PGCE courses include a compulsory music element the amount of time allocated is usually no more than about 20 hours! In most Bachelor of Education programmes students are required to follow compulsory (non-main) arts courses, although it is clear that there are sizeable numbers who receive little or no musical training. Where they do, time devoted to music, over three or four years, is not substantial. One of the main recommendations of the report is that the arts subjects should be given greater prominence in the initial training of primary school teachers; there is a shortage of teachers with sufficient expertise to ensure that all pupils receive a proper grounding in the discipline.

In spite of the numerous changes brought about by the establishment of the Council for the Accreditation of Teacher Education (CATE) there has been a mounting opposition, on the part of certain individuals and pressure groups, to initial teacher education in its present forms. During the past few years there have been calls for professional training to be undertaken in schools rather than higher education institutions; the introduction of some innovatory schemes has contributed to the view that much teacher education is ineffectual and probably unnecessary.

Underpinning current criticisms is the belief that, providing a person has 'subject knowledge', teaching is a craft that can be learned by working alongside an expert. On this view teacher training should be a type of apprenticeship. Of course, many pedagogical skills are clearly acquired in this manner and there is much to commend the apprenticeship model; it is vital for music teachers in training to work alongside experienced practitioners. All forms of music making take place in a social context and part of understanding the nature of activities is to understand their context. This was certainly recognized, although perhaps not overtly, in the training of the Kappelmeister; the same principle of learning and training in context is to be found in the idea of the articled organ pupil and the orchestral trainee. The type of musician who can deal with the varied aspects of music education is probably most likely to develop many of the necessary skills and attitudes through more direct experience of typical situations.

But teachers are also required to be have *professional* knowledge which complements their academic knowledge and practical skill. This has been recognized since the nineteenth century; with the changes presently occurring in education it has become even more necessary. At one time professional knowledge was grounded in the so-called foundation disciplines and directly related to pedagogy. It focused on theories of learning, child development and philosophical issues concerned with aims and values. Although in the past this sort of knowledge was not always sufficiently related to practice it is nevertheless of the greatest significance. Teaching within the context of education *is* value laden; it is highly complex and involves more than technique. But now teachers are required to make many more managerial and administrative decisions. There is a new body of professional knowledge. It cannot all be learned during courses of initial training and there are calls for greater INSET provision that will enable teachers to cope with the demands of their changing roles.

The importance of initial education and training is that it provides the first opportunity for intending teachers to relate academic, professional and practical knowledge in a meaningful way and to understand the broad context of teaching. Present patterns are not without faults and limitations, but to return to a system in which practical and professional knowledge are developed entirely within the school would be shortsighted, particularly in view of the complexity of the teacher's role.[16]

Conclusions

One of the most unsatisfactory aspects of music in schools is the division between the curriculum and extracurricular activities. In an age of competition and accountability there is always the danger that music beyond the classroom will overshadow the main curriculum programme. Nevertheless, concerts, plays and productions have an important educational function. It would be a great loss if these activities had to be discontinued, but this will happen if too much is expected of music teachers. Of course, public presentations do not have to be the *St. Matthew Passion* or *My Fair Lady*. Whilst there is a place for the 'big' production there is also much value in 'small scale' events involving, say, a year group or a number of classes performing work learned in timetabled lessons. These might include something like a concert of pupils' compositions or choral items that have been prepared over a period of time. Such occasions will probably not attract huge audiences but they will be of interest to the parents of those children taking part. In many schools this seems to be an increasingly popular policy; it is a manageable and educationally desirable means of combining the two traditions of music education. Curriculum and extracurricular activities will both be strengthened if they are regarded as *complementary* dimensions of the one enterprise.

There is a problem of under-staffing for music in both primary and secondary schools. This has to be considered urgently if music is to be properly developed as a foundation subject. The uncertainty over the future of instrumental tuition in schools is also a cause for great concern. So much has been achieved in this area; it would be a major tragedy and a disgrace if this aspect of music education were allowed to fall into decline and perhaps disappear altogether.

With changes taking place in arts education there are important questions to be addressed regarding the future of teacher education and training. I have expressed certain reservations about the appropriateness of consecutive modes as a form of training for music specialists. Of course, I am not advocating that all PGCE courses for music teachers be abandoned in favour of new B.Ed schemes. Nevertheless, there will be a need to consider how preparation for arts teaching can be modified in the light of changing philosophies and practices.

In spite of the fact that provision for music in schools is often limited there is evidence of much good practice.[17] The inclusion of music in the National Curriculum could provide a real opportunity for building on the achievements of the past fifty years. This will be dependent on the availability of necessary resources, but it is also essential that music and the arts are recognized as more than adornments; they need to be valued as forms of meaning that are central to the human condition and consequently an essential part of a liberal education.

Notes and References

1 An interesting analysis of accountability is provided by ERAUT, M. (1981) 'Accountability and Evaluation', in SIMON, B. and TAYLOR, W. (Eds) *Education in the Eighties*, London, Batsford.

2 CANNON, C. (1970) 'Some Variations on the Teacher's Role', in MUSGRAVE, P.W. (Ed.) *Sociology, History and Education*, London, Methuen.

3 TEE SOOK LENG (1984) *Choirs in Secondary Schools: A Study of Pupils' Attitudes*, Unpublished MA Dissertation, Institute of Education, University of London.

4 HARGREAVES, D. (1982) *The Challenge for the Comprehensive School*, London, Routledge.

5 *Ibid.*, p. 152.

6 RENSHAW, P. (1986) 'Towards the Changing Face of the Conservatoire Curriculum', *British Journal of Musical Education*, 3, 1, pp. 79–90.

7 See SMALL, C. (1977) *Music — Society — Education*, London, John Calder, (particularly Chapter 1).

8 See, for example, HUGHES, R. (1974) *Haydn: The Master Musician Series*, London, Dent, pp. 34–35.

9 KOESTLER, A. (1964) *The Act of Creation*, London, Hutchinson.

10 GUILFORD, J.P. (1975) 'Creativity: A Quarter Century of Progress', in TAYLOR, I. and GETZELS, J. (Ed.) *Perspectives in Creativity*, Chicago, Aldine.

11 Quoted in BRACE, G. (1970) *Music in the Secondary School Timetable*, Themes in Education, 24. University of Exeter.

12 LAWTON, D. (1983) *Curriculum Studies and Educational Planning*, London, Hodder and Stoughton, p. 97.

13 PAYNTER, J. (1982) *Music in The Secondary School Curriculum*, Cambridge, Cambridge University Press, p. 69.

14 In Finland, for example, where specialist music teachers are educated and trained at the Sibelius Academy, Helsinki, and the School of Music, University of Jyvaskyla. Information supplied by Professor Ellen Urho, formerly Rector of the Sibelius Academy and Professor Matti Vainio of the University of Jyvaskyla.

15 CLEAVE, S. and SHARPE, C. (1986) *The Arts: A Preparation to Teach*, Slough, National Foundation for Educational Research.

16 See SWANWICK, K. and CHITTY, C. (1989) *Research Report: Teacher Education and the PGCE*, Institute of Education, University of London.

17 See PAYNTER, J. (1982) *op. cit.*

Chapter 7

The Teaching of Music: Towards 2000

Introduction

One of the important outcomes of the 1944 Education Act was that it created a climate for the realization of those liberal ideals enshrined in the earlier Hadow and Norwood reports. Although the emergent tripartite system resulted in a certain inequality regarding access to particular kinds of knowledge, there was a gradual acceptance of the principle that children were entitled to a form of education which provided for depth and breadth of experience. Within this framework the arts were recognized as important for *all* pupils and they thus become more firmly established as curriculum subjects. These developments led subsequently to an expansion of Local Education Authority music services and the introduction of new courses of teacher training for music specialists.[1] There was good reason to believe that music would assume greater significance in pupils' education; and to some extent this belief was justified.

However, during the years following the act music teachers attending in-service courses and Local Authority meetings frequently found themselves discussing the rather uncertain status of their subject. Many acknowledged that musical contributions to the 'life of the school', through extracurricular activities, were appreciated by colleagues and parents; but teachers often felt that their work (especially in the classroom) was not regarded too seriously. The attitude of the educational establishment, so it appeared, was that the absence of music in a school would be an unfortunate and regrettable omission but not a cause for great concern. Pupils could manage without music and would not suffer any sort of educational deprivation. This was certainly not the position taken in all schools but the low-status image of the subject was noted in the Newsom Report.[2] And it became clear from the Schools Council Inquiry 1 (1968)[3] that large numbers of pupils also help music in low esteem. According to the Inquiry many secondary school pupils viewed music not only as one of the most 'useless' but also one of the most 'boring' of curriculum subjects. In response to these disappointing and somewhat alarming findings the Schools Council Music Committee promptly set up a working party to review the situation. At the time there were various rumours about the future of music in schools; some people predicted its demise as a curriculum subject, particularly at secondary level.

But in spite of its often seemingly precarious position music has survived. There have been numerous innovations and positive achievements in class music programmes as a result of new rationales, the dissemination of alternative pedagogies, the influence of Schools Council Projects and Local Authority Initiatives and, most significantly, the determination and enthusiasm of countless dedicated teachers. Although present provision is still far from ideal, music as a curriculum subject is almost certainly viewed with greater respect than it was forty years ago. But what of the future of music in schools? Can the advances made actually be sustained and further developed?

My intention in this final chapter is to discuss these questions in the light of preceding views and arguments. Quite clearly, progress in music education will be dependent on the importance attached to arts subjects and the conditions under which they are taught. The inclusion of music as a foundation subject in the National Curriculum initially provided grounds for optimism. Now that it has been designated as an option for pupils between the ages of 14 and 16 its future seems less secure. One might conclude that after all the curriculum decisions of the past five years nothing has really changed.

The Position of Music and the Arts

The 1988 Education Reform Act is a massive piece of legislation which is bound to have far-reaching effects on all aspects of education in this country. According to Stuart Sexton, one-time adviser to a former Secretary of State for Education and presently director of the education unit at the Institute of Economic Affairs, 'the current reforms are only a staging post along the way to transforming the British education system'.[4] Sexton forecasts that by the year 2000 the Department of Education and the Local Authorities will be superfluous with schools operating independently and subject entirely to market forces. He predicts that there will continue to be a national curriculum; but this will be determined by customers' (i.e. parents') demands with the focus largely on what are now the core subjects.

Professional educationists will react differently to these speculations. From the point of view of organization and administration some will welcome freedom from what is seen as Local Authority bureaucracy; others will regret the decline of a machinery which provides the various support services. Instrumental tuition schemes, music centres, holiday music courses, resources collections; all of these services have obviously had an impact on the development of music in schools. They are often taken for granted, but without them there can be little doubt that the range of musical activities and opportunities would be greatly reduced. If in this 'new' society the curriculum becomes largely a response to customer demand, and if these demands are mostly for the 'three Rs' and vocational training, then one could be forgiven for forecasting a rather dismal future for arts education. But if we ever do reach the point where the curriculum is completely under the control of 'customers' (which for a variety of reasons is most improbable) there is no reason to believe that *everybody* in society is thoroughly materialistic and looking for a type of education geared entirely to utilitarian ends. There are other views of education and alternative concepts of the good life and the good society.

If people really want schools to be places where pupils acquire only knowledge that can be used for purely instrumental purposes, then presumably that is what they will get. However, unlike Stuart Sexton I am by no means convinced that this is the will of the majority. From my own experience of teaching in very different schools I would say that parents are looking for much more than this for their children. No matter how much emphasis is placed on qualifications and vocational preparation there remains an expectation that schools will provide for a variety of experiences and a broad curriculum. There is a demand for music and the arts in schools. Nevertheless, there is still much misunderstanding over the nature of arts education, and there is also some indifference and even opposition to the arts.

I agree with Marian Metcalfe[5] when she says that the arguments in support of music have *not* been won. Mrs. Metcalfe makes her observation as a practising teacher; through daily contacts with colleagues in schools one is very aware that many still encounter and have to tolerate some negative attitudes which do much to undermine and devalue their work.[6] Some of these attitudes might be expressed fairly mildly — 'music is just fun' — but there will be some parents, members of the public and perhaps other staff within schools who do not hold the arts in high regard. There remains a certain body of opinion that perpetuates a view of the arts as unnecessary frills and distractions which get in the way of more 'serious' curriculum subjects. What is not known is how extensive these attitudes might be; but many teachers will be aware of their existence.

Those who advocate an extension of arts education are not making the naive claim that there should simply be more music and drama and less science and mathematics in educational programmes. What is being challenged is a system which often restricts pupils' vision of the world. It is a system so dominated by a particular view of knowledge, experience and understanding that children are actually being *prevented* from developing their full range of abilities, interests and potentialities. To attempt to raise the status of music and the arts within the curriculum may be seen as part of a wider exercise concerned with asking some fundamental questions not only about education but ultimately about society itself.

Signs of Changing Attitudes

Although there have been many policy changes in education since the 1944 Act, certain basic underlying assumptions about what is valuable, important and worthwhile remain unaltered; this is only too apparent from the view of knowledge which is embodied in the National Curriculum. In fact, it is quite remarkable that, in spite of all the studies and reports in connection with the content of the curriculum, the present formulation is so traditional in its structure. The point is that changes in educational attitudes, practices and policies are slow and evolutionary; they are dependent on many different factors. In considering the position of the arts in education I think it would be wrong to assume that educators can adopt any single course of action that will lead to major revisions in educational thinking and outlook. Certainly innovatory approaches to teaching, or the introduction of new equipment and materials, might be influential in bringing about significant changes in practice within a particular curriculum subject. We have seen, for example, several different influences — the 'creativity movement', an increased interest in different types of popular music, the development of acoustic and electronic instruments and the introduction of computers. All of these have had a bearing on the conduct of music education. But more fundamental views of education and attitudes towards the arts are likely to occur only over a longer period of time.

I have maintained that the increase in writings on music education during the post-war years has contributed to a greater awareness of the value of music and the arts and their place in a broad educational programme. However, the amount of literature, in this country, is sparse by comparison with that in other curriculum areas such as Science, Mathematics and the Humanities. Music educators have tended to concentrate on the production of classroom materials and books concerned with teaching methods. There has been little reference to issues in the more general field of educational studies. Writing in the *Music Education Review* of 1977 Keith Swanwick suggested that music educators were not keeping abreast of educational thinking:

> To read through articles in the music education journals and to scan the books that advocate classroom practice is to enter a world that has apparently never assimilated the

thinking of people who have influenced and still influence the climate of educational thought and practice.[7]

Of course, the situation has changed during the past decade; music is no longer what Swanwick called an 'educational island'. Nevertheless, it is very easy for those working in arts education to forget just how little of the literature actually filters through to teachers of other disciplines and the educational community. There is a need for music educators to be involved in the wider educational debate. To participate in his debate is to raise some basic questions and put forward some alternative viewpoints. For example, a consideration of changing views of knowledge and intelligence, discussed in Chapter 2, does not merely provide evidence to 'prove' that music is valuable and more significant than is generally assumed by decision makers. These alternative philosophical and psychological perspectives lead to a challenging of long held beliefs and assumptions about the curriculum which shape the course of educational policy and practice.

But promoting educational ideals is not simply an intellectual or academic task; it is also a *political* task. David Hargreaves[8] makes this point when referring to the work of Raymond Williams, whose visionary writings are much respected by educationists and highly pertinent to the development of education in a democratic society. Why, asks Hargreaves, have these views failed to have any marked influence on the development of educational policy and the curriculum? He argues that this is because bringing about change in education is determined in complex ways by different interest groups.

To talk about the politics of the curriculum is to refer to the issue of social and educational control rather than party politics, although the two are not entirely unrelated. Until fairly recently the control of the curriculum has been largely determined by the combined forces of the Department of Education, The Local Education Authorities and the teachers. Professional bodies have also been influential; organizations like the Incorporated Society of Musicians and the Schools Music Association have frequently been consulted by government ministers and civil servants in connection with policy matters. With the moves away from 'partnership' to greater central direction of the curriculum, culminating in the 1988 Act, there is an increasing realization that educators have to enter the political arena, perhaps with a greater sense of urgency, in order to pursue their aims. It is probably the case that arts educators, and particularly musicians, have been less inclined to this than other educationists. However, during the past few years we have seen much greater public and political activity on the part of professional associations. The formation of new bodies such as the National Association for Education in the Arts (NAEA), the United Kingdom Council for Music Education and Training (UKCMET) and the Association for the Advancement of Teacher Education in Music (AATEM) is symptomatic of a move towards a new and more organized professional discourse and greater involvement in curriculum issues.

These professional associations perform a number of important functions. One of their major concerns is to promote music and the arts within education and society. But they also provide a forum, through courses and conferences, for teachers, academic educationists, inspectors and administrators to come together to deliberate on a wide range of issues. In this way these organizations break down the barriers between people working in different branches of education, thus promoting a greater sense of unity amongst those concerned with the same broad field. Most importantly, the associations are a mouthpiece for arts education and have become one of the main agencies in focusing public attention on the significance of the arts. During the past few years they have provided a vital link between the professionals and the government. Much time has been devoted to the monitoring of the copious policy statements issued by the Department of Education and Science and the National Curriculum Council (NCC). The collation of views and information which is then passed on to decision-making bodies has proved to be an important means of ensuring that valued principles and practices are recognized and safeguarded. The expansion of the professional associations is one of the most positive moves towards highlighting the arts and improving their status within education.

Theory and Practice

In seeking to promote their views within the broader educational context it is, of course, important that music educators avoid making claims for music which cannot be properly substantiated. All theoretical positions and ideologies are problematic and open to further inquiry, and the educational climate is one in which ideas are subject to rigorous scrutiny and hence rejection (and even ridicule) if they are shown to be fanciful and without adequate foundation. Principles of justification are a case in point.

Because of its weak status as a curriculum subject, there has been a tendency to advance all sorts of reasons for the inclusion of music in a general education; some of these justifications have not been backed up by suitable arguments or appropriate evidence. A typical example of an unsupported and consequently unhelpful justification is that regular music study leads to improved performance in other areas of the curriculum. At one time this view seemed to receive support from certain Hungarian music educators.[9] It was maintained there was 'overwhelming evidence' to show that pupils attending the special music primary schools (where they receive at least one hour of musical instruction each day) attained much higher general academic standards than did their contemporaries in the normal primary schools. The conclusion drawn was that music has some special 'educative power' which could be of benefit to all children. This evidence appeared to stake a claim for music which could hardly be challenged by anybody who was genuinely concerned about children's educational development. But no thought was given to existing psychological theories and research findings relating to the transfer of learning; in fact, psychological evidence raises serious doubts about these claims. It is well known that musical studies in the Hungarian music schools are highly organized and that pupils are strongly motivated and committed to an educational style which emphasizes success and achievement. Studies of transfer indicate that what is likely to lead to good overall performance is the transfer of appropriate study habits and positive attitudes towards learning; and, of course, these can be acquired through any discipline.[10] There is no precise empirical evidence to suggest that music itself has some magical property which will lead to children performing better in history, science, mathematics or anything else.

But leaving aside the unsatisfactory basis of the argument, the justification for music in these terms becomes one which emphasizes its instrumental value. We see signs of this type of view creeping into current educational thinking; it is sometimes maintained that, through music, pupils develop certain mental qualities or 'excellencies' like divergent thinking or imaginativeness, and even agreeable dispositions such as concentration, tolerance and perseverance; all of these qualities, so it is said, are the very things that employers are looking for. Again, arguments of this nature are very tenuous. Tolerance, for example, is an attitude we would look for in any educational activity; it is not peculiar to music any more than is the ability to concentrate or the need to persevere. Divergent thinking in music is very different from divergent thinking in engineering or cookery; there is no reason to believe that cognitive styles transfer from one discipline to another or from one form of intelligence to another. Some of these misguided views are used to support the idea of music as a 'servicing subject'.[11] Not only are the arguments totally unfounded but they detract from the significance of music as a realm of meaning in its own right. The study of music and other arts subjects may well contain elements which contribute to an understanding of information technology, to personal and social education and to vocational preparation. But if these become the main reasons for including music in the curriculum then its *aesthetic* value is likely to be diminished or lost altogether. To dwell on the 'servicing' potential of music is to adopt a very precarious position; rather than advancing music education, extrinsic justifications may well have just the opposite effect. As we have seen, all justifications imply a particular form of practice. Using music to service other areas of the curriculum can easily lead to practices that are just as aesthetically sterile as the old type of musicological studies.

In Chapter 1 I referred to different conceptions and practices of music education which arise from alternative views, or theories, of education. Stated rather crudely, traditionalists emphasize the importance of conventional techniques, the Post-Renaissance Classical tradition and the preservation of what is called the cultural heritage; progressive educators tend to focus on feeling, interests, relevance, discovery and self-expression. Although it would be mistaken to suggest that there are easily definable camps, alternative music education practices associated with these positions have sometimes been the cause of strong disagreements. I have already referred to Ross, Witkin, Vulliamy and Small (Chapter 3) who, in their different ways, have been highly critical of much traditional teaching. On the other side Peter Fletcher[12] and Arnold Bentley[13] claim that certain progressive approaches and innovations can easily misrepresent and devalue the discipline of music.

But there has also been marked tendency towards the establishment of a middle ground. Bernarr Rainbow,[14] for example, is a very outspoken critic of those progressive educators who ignore the importance of choral activities and the development of aural and literacy skills. Nevertheless he advocates the bringing together of different types of music teaching within a cohesive framework. Similarly, John Paynter, often regarded as a more progressive music educationist, has never been exclusive in his views of practice and has frequently emphasized the misunderstandings that have arisen in connection with 'creative music'. He too has argued in favour of uniting both tradition and innovation in music education. In fact, Paynter and Aston's celebrated book *Sound and Silence*[15] is representative of this principle. Although published twenty years ago it remains one of the best examples of an inclusive approach to music teaching which incorporates past and present in a highly imaginative manner.

It might be possible to identify a few schools where practices are based on extreme forms of either traditionalism or progressivism. And one does occasionally meet people whose ideas about aims, content and teaching styles are so determined by methodological ideals that they become extremely intransigent in both theory and practice. But disagreements in music education are largely ideological. The reality of practice is that most teachers work out practices which they consider to be most suitable in particular circumstances; they adopt strategies which incorporate both conventional and experimental forms of music making. In some instances this may be a question of teacher survival in the sense of finding anything that 'works' with disaffected pupils, but more often than not it is a matter of realizing the vast range of musical representation and the wide variety of possible activity.

An eclectic or conservationist pedagogy appeals to teachers because it entails certain musical principles which they understand and value. Most teachers, as practising musicians, recognize and embrace the great traditions; but musicians are also used to innovation and are highly tolerant of experimentation. In Chapter 3 I referred to Sir Adrian Boult's attitude towards music and I think this exemplifies the world view of musicians generally. They respect and value tradition but are prepared to try new works without being constrained by preconceived notions of what music *should* be. As I said earlier, there is a difference in attitude and commitment between the music enthusiast and the professional musician. When working with amateur groups one is often struck by how *conservative* many people are in their musical tastes. Amongst choralists, for example, there will be those who will never miss a rehearsal of *Messiah*, but ask them to sing the music of Poulenc, Kodaly or David Fanshawe and some will simply stay away.

However, within education, the eclecticism of conservationism is not simply a matter of selecting from traditional and progressive repertoires and methodologies. It involves developing forms of practice that are based on the principle of music as a meaningful form of human experience and not a type of entertainment or relaxation. Musical *understanding* is its watchword; the aim is to enable children to enter the world of music so that they will come to an awareness of those deep structures which convey meanings across a wide variety of styles and genres. In no way does this imply conformity in practice. Indeed, it allows for diversity but within a common framework that emphasizes the great *continuum* which is the aesthetic field of music.

Organizational Conditions and Constraints

Obviously, all educational practice will be determined by the conditions under which it takes place. Indeed, it is often said that the successful implementation of curricula is always dependent on four factors: accommodation, staffing, time and financial resources. Of these, the two that militate most strongly against the development of comprehensive and coherent programmes are teacher supply and the allocation of curriculum time.

I have expressed reservations (in Chapters 4 and 6) about the current situation in those primary schools where present policy often seems to be directed more towards 'coping' rather than laying foundations. Certainly, reforms in teacher education could do much to alleviate this problem. And, of course, there are many excellent schemes already in operation designed to assist general class teachers and to improve provision for music education in the primary sector. But it may be that there is a need for alternative and innovative patterns of staffing. One forward-looking recommendation proposed by Marjorie Glynne-Jones[16] is the notion of 'community staffing'. Miss Glynne-Jones has argued that practical organizational problems have to be faced and alternative models are required if we are to adapt effectively to changing circumstances. Central to community staffing would be a commitment to collaborative team-based teaching. For example, a team of specialist music teachers might operate in a secondary school, a number of associated primary schools and also work with youth organizations and in adult education. Such an arrangement would not only ensure that greater numbers of pupils received proper education in music but it could also be a way of improving coherence, progression and continuity in curriculum practice. Exactly how such a plan would operate in the light of financial, legal and logistic factors would obviously require detailed planning, but this type of thoughtful proposal could be one way of tackling the serious problem of teacher shortage.

Many teachers would probably be of the opinion that one of the most frustrating organizational constraints they have to contend with is the small amount of time given to the music curriculum. The Gulbenkian Committee[17] referred to the inappropriateness of the single weekly period of 30–40 minutes for a discipline which requires regular study, if pupils are to develolp a progressive understanding. It does not follow that limited time necessarily leads to meaningless experience, but a broad and inclusive programme can never be effectively implemented until the issue of time allocation is given proper consideration.

I am very much in agreement with those who argue in favour of blocking arts subjects (in secondary schools) with members of the arts team working together on curriculum planning, structure and practice. But there has to be a *reasonable* amount of time. It has been recommended, in *Living Powers*,[18] that as much as one-third of curriculum time should be devoted to arts subjects. At first sight this may not seem feasible. But the proposal is based on the notion of the six arts — music, literature, visual art, drama, dance, film and television studies — as a generic community concerned primarily with aesthetic knowledge. They are not regarded as isolated disciplines, parts of other disciplines or servicing subjects. Looked at in this way the proposal is not unrealistic; it would not require a radical reorganization of the timetable. The major requirement is a reconception of the arts subjects themselves.

In addition to these specific problems of staffing and time allocation there are the present bureaucratic demands on teachers. These frequently obstruct teaching across the curriculum. Teachers have always been concerned with curriculum planning, assessment, innovation and development strategies. But as a result of government policies they now find themselves submerged in a sea of paper concerned with statutory orders, non-statutory advice, guides to assessment, Local Education Authority policy statements and many other matters. All of this inevitably distracts teachers from their main task of *educating children*. There is also much uncertainty brought by constant changes in policy. At one point we were told that implementation of music for Key Stage 4 was to be brought forward from 1995 to 1992. A few weeks later, 1995 was reinstated as the correct date. And now music is no longer a compulsory element for the 14 to 16 age group! The avowed aim of the education reformers is to improve teaching and learning and thereby raise standards. But the present government initiatives have over-burdened and confused teachers. Unless it is recognized that there must be a limit to administrative duties, the quality of teaching and learning will be seriously endangered, not only in the arts but in all areas of the curriculum.

Conclusions

One of the findings of a research study carried out at the London Institute of Education in 1987[19] was that music appeared to be more highly regarded in schools than might have been expected. A detailed survey of twenty-three secondary and nine primary schools revealed that teachers (of all subjects) and non-teaching staff (caretakers, secretaries, librarians, cleaners) showed great interest in concerts, plays, carol services and other extracurricular activities involving music and the arts. They welcomed these events as contributions to the cultural life of the school. Naturally, it would be unwise to draw any general conclusions from such a small-scale inquiry but the findings do seem to be consistent with the commonly-held view that music is valued to the extent that corporate activities add to a sense of unity and social cohesion.

But if music is to be a potent force in the education of pupils it must also be in a healthy state as a curriculum subject. And this will ultimately be dependent on a recognition of the arts as realms of meaning, equal in significance to those forms of understanding which have traditionally occupied pride of place in an unquestioned curriculum devoted to the acquisition of propositional knowledge. Changing epistemologies and new conceptions of intelligence have led to a re-awakening of the fact that there are important ways of knowing which do not rely solely on discursive language. In all societies we find aesthetic languages and systems, for, as Dewey maintained, to make and respond to art works is basic to the human condition. People seek artistic experience not merely for amusement. They employ aesthetic forms of thinking (with linguistic, mathematical and other forms) for the purpose of ordering and making sense of their complex worlds. And for this reason the arts have a vital position in a liberal education for all children.

It is against this background that I have argued for a systematic and properly planned music curriculum based on a broad conception of music and musical activity. Pupils will need to have wide experiences which will enable them to learn the skills, techniques and procedures of the discipline and to discover the world of music in all its diversity. But however well planned curricula might be, initiation into the arts can never be achieved through slavishly following prescribed outlines and meeting predetermined targets set out in documents. It is the process and quality of experience, governed by the nature of the discipline itself, that is at the heart of meaningful educational encounters. And improvement in practice is dependent on the study of practice. Teachers need time to reflect on the complexitites of the classroom and to contemplate educational success and failure. It is through self–critical analysis of practice and the sharing of pedagogical information in professional dialogue that music teachers will gain a greater understanding of their field. Music education is a practical enterprise informed by a range of theoretical perspective; its development depends on the fusion of theory and practice.

Throughout this book I have referred to the various problems of music education and the difficulties which confront teachers in the course of their professional work. Negative attitudes towards the arts, shortages of teachers, poor facilities, lack of time, inadequate accommodation — any of these factors can have a deleterious effect on the practice of music teaching. Some teachers have to put up with intolerable conditions, and even a few minor practical reforms would often do much to improve the teaching and learning environment; on occasion conditions are so limiting it is a wonder that any music *education* is possible at all. I want to emphasize these points because they are so important and teachers rightly complain that such issues are frequently overlooked in writings on education; hence my colleagues' sceptical remarks referred to at the beginning of Chapter 1.

Many advances in music education have been made because of the enthusiasm and commitment of teachers who are prepared to work round practical obstacles; they believe in the value of their subject and what they are trying to achieve. As long as there is this enthusiasm and so much good will there is every reason to remain optimistic about the future of music in education. And, of course, there are a large number of schools where music is regarded as an important aspect of pupils' general education and is given full support. Indeed, it is always a pleasure to visit schools where arts activities are in evidence, adding a certain vibrant quality to the atmosphere of the institution. And this is the power of the arts. As I have said earlier, schools without arts programmes would be dreary places. They would lack those cultural and expressive qualities which are vital aspects of a truly liberal education and essential dimensions of the good life. I can think of no better way of emphasizing this point than by quoting Professor David Aspin who, in rejecting utilitarian conceptions of education, has conveyed the message of this book and the message of the present series:

> ... the arts give us a point of reference and a sense of identification with our society and its culture, an awareness of our roots, of the richness of what is and of the complexities of what might be, with untold illuminations of objects and people that transform our view of them and so significantly alter our world ... they enable us to transcend the pragmatic preoccupations of the struggle for existence, to dignify our lives and beautify our surroundings, to add innumerable possibilities of vividness, intensity and personal enrichment to the existence of all.[20]

Notes and References

1 RAINBOW, B. (1985) *Onward from Butler. School Music 1945–1985*, London, Curwen Institute.
2 CENTRAL ADVISORY COUNCIL FOR EDUCATION (1963) *Half Our Future*, London, HMSO, para. 414,420.
3 SCHOOLS COUNCIL (1968) *Inquiry 1. Young School Leavers*, London, HMSO, Chapter 3.

4 SEXTON, S. (1990) 'Education 2000. Free Markets, better Values', *Education Guardian*, 15 August, 1990.

5 METCALFE, M. (1987) 'Towards the Condition of Music', in ABBS, P. (Ed.) *Living Powers, The Arts in Education*, London, Falmer Press, pp. 97–118.

6 *Ibid.*

7 SWANWICK, K. (1987) 'Belief and Action in Music Education', in BURNETT, M. (Ed.) *Music Education Review*, 1, London, Chappell, pp. 63–82.

8 HARGREAVES, D. (1982) *The Challenge for the Comprehensive School*, London, Routledge and Kegan Paul, Chapter 8.

9 FRIGYES, S. (1966) *Musical Education in Hungary*, London, Boosey and Hawkes.

10 A useful account of psychological theories of transfer is to be found in KLAUSMEIER, H. (1975) *Learning and Human Abilities*, London, Harper and Row.

11 See, for example, DOLEY, M. *et al.* (1978) Music in the Curriculum, London, Lancashire Education Committee.

12 FLETCHER, P. (1987) *Education and Music*, Oxford, Oxford University Press.

13 BENTLEY, A. (1975) *Music in Education: A Point of View*, Slough, National Foundation for Educational Research.

14 RAINBOW, B. (1985) *op. cit.*

15 PAYNTER, J. and ASTON, P. (1970) *Sound and Silence*, Cambridge, Cambridge University Press.

16 See ASSOCIATION FOR THE ADVANCEMENT OF TEACHER EDUCATION IN MUSIC (1986) *Newsletter 5*, Spring, pp. 4–5.

17 GULBENKIAN FOUNDATION (1982) *The Arts in Schools*, Gulbenkian Foundation, p. 63.

18 ABBS, P. (1987) (Ed.) *Living Powers: the Arts in Education*, London, Falmer Press, p. 209.

19 SWANWICK, K. *et al.* (1987) *Music in Schools: A Study of Context and Curriculum Practice*, Institute of Education, University of London.

20 ASPIN, D. (1981) 'Utility is not Enough: The Arts in the School Curriculum', in WHITE, J. (Ed.) *No Minister: A Critique of the DES Paper, the School Curriculum*, Bedford Way Papers No. 4, London, Kogan Page.

Bibliography

Abbs, P. (1987) (Ed.) *Living Powers: The Arts in Education*, London, Falmer Press.

Abbs, P. (1989) (Ed.) *The Symbolic Order*, London, Falmer Press.

Addison, R. (1986) 'The Arts in Education', Arts Initiatives 1, London, National Association for Education in the Arts.

Allen, D. (1988) 'Models of Combined Arts Practice', in SCHOOL CURRICULUM DEVELOPMENT COMMITTEE, *Combined Arts in Secondary Schools, op. cit.*

Aspin D. (1981) 'Utility is not Enough: The Arts in the School Curriculum', in White, J. (Ed.) *No Minister: A Critique of the DES Paper, The School Curriculum, op. cit.*

Aspin, D. (1984) *Objectivity and Assessment in the Arts The Problem of Aesthetic Education*, National Association for Education in the Arts.

Association for the Advancement of Teacher Education in Music (1986) *Newsletter 5*, Spring.

Bennett, S. (1976) 'The Process of Musical Creation', *Journal of Research in Music Education*, 24, 1, pp. 3–31.

Bentley, A. (1966) *Musical Ability in Children and its Measurement*, Harrap.

Bentley, A. (1975) *Music in Education: A Point of View*, Slough, NFER.

Ben-Tovim, A. (1979) *Children and Music*, London, A.C. Black.

Bernstein, B. (1971) 'On the Classification and Framing of Knowledge', in Young, M.F.D., *Knowledge and Control: New Directions for the Sociology of Knowledge, op. cit.*

BEST, D. (1989) 'Feeling and Reason in the Arts: The Rationality of Feeling', in ABBS, P. (Ed.) *The Symbolic Order, op. cit.*

BLACKING, J. (1973) *How Musical is Man?* London, Faber.

BLACKING, J. (1986) *Culture and the Arts*, London, National Association for Education in the Arts.

BOARD OF EDUCATION (1922) 'Report on Music Teaching in Secondary Schools', Circular 1252.

BRACE, G. (1970) *Music and the Secondary School Timetable*, Themes in Education 24, University of Exeter.

BRUNER, J. (1963) *The Process of Education*, New York, Vintage Books.

BRUNER, J.S. (1966) *Toward a Theory of Instruction*, New York, Norton.

BURNETT, M. (Ed.) (1977) *Music Education Review*, 1, London, Chappell.

CALOUST GULBENKIAN FOUNDATION (1982) *The Arts in Schools*, London, Caloust Gulbenkian Foundation.

CANNON, C. (1970) 'Some Variations on the Teachers Role', in MUSGRAVE, P.W. (Ed.) *Sociology, History and Education, op. cit.*

CENTRAL ADVISORY COUNCIL FOR EDUCATION (1963) *Half Our Future*, London, HMSO.

CLEAVE, S. and SHARPE, C. (1986) *The Arts: A Preparation to Teach*, Slough, NFER.

COLWELL, R. (1970) *The Evaluation of Music Teaching and Learning*, Englewood Cliffs, Prentice Hall.

COOKE, D. (1959) *The Language of Music*, Oxford, Oxford University Press.

CRAFT, A. and BARDELL, G. (Eds) (1984) *Curriculum Opportunities in A Multi-Cultural Society*, London, Harper and Row.

DEARDEN, R.F., HIRST, P.H. and PETERS, R.S. (Eds) (1972) *Education and the Development of Reason*, London, Routledge.

DEPARTMENT OF EDUCATION AND SCIENCE (1981) *Aesthetic Development: A Report from the Assessment of Performance Unit, Exploratory Group on Aesthetic Development*, Department of Education and Science.

DEPARTMENT OF EDUCATION AND SCIENCE (1985) *Music from 5 to 16*, Curriculum Matters 4, London, HMSO.

DEPARTMENT OF EDUCATION AND SCIENCE (1985) *General Certificate of Secondary Education: The National Criteria: Music*, London, HMSO.

DEPARTMENT OF EDUCATION AND SCIENCE (1987) *National Curriculum: Task Group on Assessment and Testing: A Report*, London, Department of Education and Science.

DEPARTMENT OF EDUCATION AND SCIENCE (1989) *Standards in Education, 1988–89. The Annual Report of HM Senior Chief Inspector of Schools*, London, HMSO.

DEWEY, J. (1958) *Art as Experience*, New York, Capricorn Books. (first published 1934).

DOBBS, J. and SHEPHERD, F. (1984) 'Music', in CRAFT, A. and BARDELL, G. (Eds) *Curriculum Opportunities in A Multi-Cultural Society, op. cit.*

DOLEY, M. (1978) *Music in the Curriculum*, Lancashire Education Committee.

ELLIS, A. (1982) *Normality and Pathology in Cognitive Functions*, London, Academic Press.

ERAUT, M. (1981) 'Accountability and Evaluation', in SIMON, B. and TAYLOR, W. (Eds) *Education in the Eighties, op. cit.*

FAWCETT, B. (1981) *The Gloucester Evaluation of Time for For Music*, University of Reading School of Education.

FLETCHER, P. (1987) *Education and Music*, Oxford, Oxford University Press.

FRIGYES, S. (1966) *Musical Education in Hungary*, London, Boosey and Hawkes.

GAGNE, R. (1985) *The Conditions of Learning*, 5th ed., New York, Holt, Reinhart and Winston.

GAMBLE, T. (1982) 'Music and the integration of the arts', in PAYNTER, J. *Music in the Secondary School Curriculum, op. cit.*

GARDNER, H. (1982) '*Artistry following Damage to the Human Brain*', in ELLIS, A. (Ed.) *Normality and Pathology in Cognitive Functions, op. cit.*

GARDNER, H. (1984) *Frames of Mind: The Theory of Multiple Intelligences*, London, Heinemann.

GRIERSON, D. (1980) 'An Investigation into some factors affecting the attitudes of a group of thirteen-year-old children towards music', Unpublished M.A. Dissertation, University of London, Institute of Education.

GUILFORD, J.P. (1975) 'Creativity: A Quarter Century of Progress', in TAYLOR, I. and GETZELS, J. (Eds) *Perspectives in Creativity, op. cit.*

HAMLYN, D. (1972) 'Objectivity', in DEARDEN, R.F., HIRST, P.H. and PETERS, R.S. (Eds) *Education and the Development of Reason, op. cit.*

HARGREAVES, D.J. (1986) *The Developmental Psychology of Music,* Cambridge, Cambridge University Press.

HARGREAVES, D.H. (1982) *The Challenge for the Comprehensive School,* London, Routledge.

HILL, K. (1983) *The Secondary School Intake and the Music Curriculum,* Unpublished M.A. Dissertation, Institute of Education, University of London.

HINDEMITH, P. (1952) *A Composer's World,* Gloucester, Mass., Harvard University Press.

HIRST, P. (1974) *Knowledge and the Curriculum,* London, Routledge.

HOGGART, R. (1973) *Speaking to Each Other,* 1, Harmondsworth, Penguin.

HUGHES, R. (1974) *Haydn: The Master Musician Series,* London, Dent.

INCORPORATED SOCIETY OF MUSICIANS (1947) *An Outline of Musical Education,* London, Curwen.

KENDELL, L. (1976) 'If you can teach reading you can teach music', *Schools Council Dialogue,* No. 22, London, Schools Council, pp. 8–9.

KENDELL, I. (1976) *Time for Music: Teachers' Support Book,* London, Arnold.

KELLER, H. (1966) 'Wolfgang Amadeus Mozart', in SIMPSON, R. (Ed.) *The Symphony,* 1, Harmondsworth, Pelican.

KHAN, N. (1976) *The Arts Britain Ignores,* London, Community Relations Commission.

KLAUSMEIER, H. (1975) *Learning and Human Abilities,* London, Harper and Row.

KOESTLER, A. (1964) *The Act of Creation,* London, Hutchinson.

KWAMI, R. (1986) 'A West African Folktale in the Classroom', *British Journal of Music Education,* 3, 1, pp. 5–18.

LANGER, S. (1957) *Philosophy in a New Key,* 3rd. ed., Cambridge, Mass. Harvard University Press.

LAWTON, D. (1983) *Curriculum Studies and Educational Planning*, London, Hodder and Stoughton.

LAWTON, D. (1989) *Education, Culture and the National Curriculum*, London, Hodder and Stoughton.

MANHATTENVILLE MUSIC CURRICULUM PROGRAM (1970) MMCP *Synthesis*, Media Materials Inc., New York.

METCALFE, M. (1987) 'Towards the Condition of Music', in ABBS, P. (Ed.) *Living Powers, op. cit.*

MOORE, J. NORTHROP (Ed.) (1979) *Music and Friends. Letters to Sir Adrian Boult*, Hamish Hamilton.

MURPHY, W. (1968) 'Creative Music Making in the Primary School', in RAINBOW, B. (Ed.) *Music Teachers Handbook, op. cit.*

MUSGRAVE, P.W. (Ed.) (1970) *Sociology, History and Education*, London, Methuen.

NEWMAN, J.H. (1852) *The Idea of a University*, Discourse VI, (Ed. MARTIN, J.) London, Reinhart Press.

NIXON, J. (Ed.) (1981) *A Teacher's guide to Action Research*, London, Grant Mcintyre.

PAYNTER, J. (1982) *Music in the Secondary School Curriculum*, Cambridge, Cambridge University Press.

PAYNTER, J. (1989) 'The Challenge of Creativity', *British Journal of Music Education*, 6, 2, pp. 235–237.

PAYNTER, J. and ASTON, P. (1970) *Sound and Silence*, Cambridge, Cambridge University Press.

PETERS, R.S. (1966) *Ethics and Education*, London, Allen and Unwin.

PETERS, R.S. (Ed.) (1975) *The Philosophy of Education*, Oxford, Oxford University Press.

PLUMMERIDGE, C. (1981) *Issues in Music Education*, Bedford Way Paper No. 3, London, Kogan Page.

POINTON, M. (1980) 'Mucking about with noises', A reply to Aelwyn Pugh, *Cambridge Journal of Education*, 10, 1, pp. 35–39.

PRING, R. (1975) 'The Language of Curriculum Analysis', *The Curriculum: Studies in Education No. 2*, Institute of Education, University of London.

PRING, R.A. (1975) 'Curriculum Integration', in PETERS, R.S. (Ed.) *The Philosophy of Education, op. cit.*

PRING, R.A. (1976) *Knowledge and Schooling*, London, Open Books.

PUGH, A. (1980) 'In Defence of Musical Literacy', *Cambridge Journal of Education*, 10, 1, pp. 29–34.

RAINBOW, B. (1968) (Ed.) *Music Teachers Handbook*, London, Novello.

RAINBOW, B. (1985) *Onward from Butler: School Music 1945–1985*, London, Curwen Institute.

REID, L.A. (1969) *Meaning in the Arts*, London, Allen and Unwin.

REID, L.A. (1986) *Ways of Understanding and Education*, London, Heinemann.

RENSHAW, P. (1986) 'Towards the Changing Face of the Conservatoire Curriculum', *British Journal of Educational Studies*, 3, 1, pp. 79–90.

ROBINSON, G. (1988) 'Considerations on Assessment in the Arts in the Primary Sector', in NATIONAL ASSOCIATION FOR EDUCATION IN THE ARTS, *Assessment in the Arts 1*, Take-Up Series No. 7, *op. cit.*

ROSS, M. (1975) *Arts and the Adolescent*, Schools Council Working Paper No. 54, London, Evans.

SCHAFER, R. MURRAY (1975) *The Rhinoceros in the Classroom*, Ontario Universal Edition.

SCHOOLS COUNCIL (1968) *Inquiry 1. Young School Leavers*, London, HMSO.

SCHOOLS COUNCIL (1974) *Music in the Secondary Curriculum*, News Sheet One, Schools Council.

SCHOOLS COUNCIL (1981) *The Practical Curriculum*, London, Methuen.

SCHOOL CURRICULUM DEVELOPMENT COMMITTEE (1988) *Combined Arts in Secondary Schools*, Papers by the Central Team of The Arts in Schools project, School Curriculum Development Committee.

SCHOLES, P. (1947) *The Mirror of Music*, London, Novello.

SCHWAB, J. (1969) 'The Practical: A Language for Curriculum', *School Review*, 78, 1, pp. 1–23.

SCRIMSHAW, P. (1973) 'Statements, language and art: some comments on Professor Hirst's paper', *Cambridge Journal of Education*, 3, 3, p. 44.

SCRUTON, R. (1983) *The Aesthetic Understanding*, Methuen.

SEASHORE, C. (1967) *Psychology of Music*, New York, Dover Publications (first published 1938).

SERGEANT, D. and NEWMAN, C. (1989) 'Teachers as Judges in GCSE', *Psychology of Music*, 17, p. 83.

SEXTON, S. (1990) 'Education 2000: Free Markets, Better Values', *Education Guardian*, 15 August 1990.

SHEPHERD, J. (*et al.*) (1977) *Whose Music? A Sociology of Musical Languages*, London, Latimer.

SHIPMAN, M. (1974) *Inside a Curriculum Project*, Methuen.

SHUTER-DYSON, R. and GABRIEL, C. (1981) *The Psychology of Musical Ability*, 2nd. ed., London, Methuen.

SIMON, B. and TAYLOR, W. (Eds) (1984) *Education in the Eighties*, London, Batsford.

SIMPSON, K. (1975) *Some Great Music Educators*, London, Novello.

SIMPSON, R. (1966) *The Symphony*, Harmondsworth, Pelican.

SLOBODA, J. (1985) *The Musical Mind*, Oxford, Clarendon Press.

SMALL, C. (1977) *Music — Society — Education*, London, John Calder.

STENHOUSE, L. (1975) *An Introduction to Curriculum Research and Development*, London, Heinemann.

STRAVINSKY, I. and CRAFT, R. (1961) *Dialogues and a Diary*, London, Faber.

SWANWICK, K. (1977) 'Belief and Action in Music Education', in BURNETT, M. (Ed.) *Music Education Review*, 1, *op. cit.*

SWANWICK, K. (1979) *A Basis for Music Education*, Slough, NFER.

SWANWICK, K. (1988) *Music, Mind and Education*, London, Routledge.

SWANWICK, K. (Ed.) (1988) *Assessment in the Arts 1*. Take up Series, No. 7, National Association for Education in the Arts.

SWANWICK, K. (Ed.) (1988) *Assessment in the Arts 2*. Take up Series, No. 8, National Association for Education in the Arts.

SWANWICK, K. *et al.* (1987) *Music in Schools: A Study of Context and Curriculum Practice*, Institute of Education, University of London.

SWANWICK, K. and CHITTY, C. (1989) *Research Report: Teacher Education and the PGCE*, Institute of Education, University of London.

SWANWICK, K. and TILLMAN, J. (1986) 'The Sequence of Musical Development', *British Journal of Music Education*, 3, 3, pp. 305–339.

TAWNEY, D. (Ed.) (1976) *Curriculum Evaluation Today: Trends and Implications*, London, Macmillan.

TAYLOR, D. (1981) 'Towards a Theory of Musical Instruction', in PLUMMERIDGE, C. (*et al.*) *Issues in Music Education, op. cit.*

TAYLOR, D. (1986) 'Integration in the Arts', *Arts Initiatives 1*, London, National Association for Education in the Arts.

TAYLOR, I. and GETZELS, J. (Eds) (1975) *Perspectives in Creativity*, New York, Aldine.

TAYLOR, M. (1986) 'Music Profiles — A pilot Scheme', *British Journal of Music Education*, 3, 1, pp. 19–33.

TEE SOOK LENG (1984) *Choirs in Secondary Schools: A Study of Pupils Attitudes*, Unpublished M.A. Dissertation, Institute of Education, University of London.

TYLER, R. (1949) *Basic Principles of Curriculum and Instruction*, Chicago, University of Chicago Press.

VERNON, P. (1970) *Creativity*, Penguin.

VULLIAMY, G. (1977) 'Music as a Case Study in the New Sociology of Education', in SHEPHERD, J. (*et al.*) *Whose Music? A Sociology of Musical Languages, op. cit.*

VULLIAMY, G. and LEE, E. (Eds) (1976) *Pop Music in Schools*, Cambridge, Cambridge University Press.

VULLIAMY, G. and LEE, E. (Eds) (1982) *Pop, Rock and Ethnic Music*, Cambridge, Cambridge University Press.

WHITE, J.P. (1968) 'Creativity and Education: a philosophical analysis', *British Journal of Educational Studies*, 16, 2, pp. 123–127.

WHITE, J. (1973) *Towards a Compulsory Curriculum*, London, Routledge.

WHITE, J. (Ed.) (1981) *No Minister: A Critique of the DES Paper, The School Curriculum*, Bedford Way Papers No. 4, London, Kogan Page.

WILLS, G. (1980) *An Investigation into the Interests and Attitudes of Secondary School Children Towards Music: A Case Study*,

Unpublished M.A. Dissertation, Institute of Education, University of London.

WITKIN, R. (1974) *The Intelligence of Feeling*, London, Heinemann.

WITTGENSTEIN, L. (1953) *Philosophical Investigations*, London, Blackwell.

YOUNG, M.F.D. (Ed.) (1971) *Knowledge and Control: New Directions for the Sociology of Knowledge*, London, Collier-Macmillan.

Index

Abbs, Peter *ix-xiii*, 21–2, 35
accountability 93–4, 95, 106–7, 125,
 130–1: 'bureaucratic' 126–7
action research 101–7
adaptation 17, 99
Addison, Richard 61
aesthetic, the 62
aesthetic theories 33–4
alternative music education 144
amateur 82
appreciation of music 48–9
apprenticeship model of teacher
 training 129–30
Aristotle 47
arts
 commercial uses of 114–15; as
 communication systems 27–8;
 as forms of meaning and
 knowing 10, 19, 62, 148; magic
 of the 12–13; in National
 Curriculum 22; position of 119,
 136–9; status in schools 1–2, 60,
 127; value of the 150
Arts and the Adolescent (Schools
 Council) 8, 99–100
arts curriculum, place of music in
 xiii, 59–63
arts education 54, 99, 138
 dangers and difficulties of
 assessment 84–5

arts organizations 122
Arts in Schools, The (Gulbenkian
 Foundation) 54, 62, 147
arts subjects
 blocking 147; position in teacher
 education 127–30
Aspin, David 30, 150
assessment
 criterion-referenced 83; informal
 and formal 84–6; measurement
 problems 85–8; norm-
 referenced 83; principle of public
 83–4; problem of musical *xiii*,
 83–9
Assessment of Performance Unit
 (APU), Exploratory Group on
 Aesthetic Development 85–6
Association for the Advancement of
 Teacher Education in Music
 (AATEM) 141
Aston, P., *Sound and Silence* 144
attitudes, to the arts 1–2, 94–5, 121,
 149: signs of change 138–41
audition, *see* listening
Augustine, Saint 19
aural training 53
authority, teacher as 68–73

Bachelor of Education programmes
 129, 131

behavioural objectives model of
curriculum 73–8
Bentley, Arnold 36–7, 96, 144
Bernstein, Basil 60
Best, David 17
Black, Paul 84
Blacking, John 57–8
blocking, arts subjects 147
Boult, Sir Adrian 72, 145
Brace, Geoffrey 11
Brinson, Peter, *Dance as Education* xi
Bruner, J. 69, 79–80, 81
Burney, Dr 19

Cannon, C. 113
Chomsky, N. 40
class music teaching 11, 50, 111
classroom interaction 102; *see also*
action research
classroom observation 97
Cleave, Shirley 129
cognitive and affective modes 17, 20,
35
cognitive dimension of music 19
cognitive feedback 83
combined arts departments 128
combined arts programmes, music
and 59–63
commitment, sense of 72–3, 149–50
community, music in *xiii*, 111–33
community education 115–22
community of learners 67
community service 119–20
'community staffing' 146
competition between schools 94–5,
114, 130
competitions, national and
international 83
composition *xi*, 31, 47, 50–2, 77,
123: assessment of 87; group 50
computers 139
conceptual framework 8, 99–100
conditions of teaching 67–73
connoisseurship 48–9, 63
conservationist view 21–2

consumers of music 48–9, 55
Cooke, Derek 28–9
cooperative arts projects 117–18
corporate music making 114
Council for the Accreditation of
Teacher Education (CATE) 129
counterpoint 51
creativity *xii*, 38, 122–4, 139
cultural inheritance 18
curriculum 45
'collection code' 60; continuity in
the 79; and extracurriculum
112–15; implementation of
146–8; 'integrated' 60; politics of
the 140–1; and power structures
60–1; as a 'selection from the
culture' 57; 'spiral' 79–80; *see
also* National Curriculum
curriculum development
curriculum evaluation and 96–7;
slow evolution 13, 108
curriculum planning, collaborative
63
curriculum reform movement
(1960s and 1970s) 8, 95, 96
curriculum theory, and practice 74
Curwen, John 11, 27, 53, 67

Dalcroze, Emile Jaques- 67
Davies, Peter Maxwell *xii*
Davies, Walford 47
deep musical structures 58, 79–80,
145
Department of Education and
Science 140, 141
developmental models 80–1, 130
Dewey, John *xi*, 27–8, 40, 62, 148
dialogue 100, 149
discipline 103
discourse, of the arts 39–40
Dobbs, Jack 58

eclecticism 19–22, 145
education
as adaptation 99; child-centred

theories 55–6, 67; and
  worthwhile activities 18–19
Education Act (1944) 10, 135
Education Guardian 127
Education Reform Act (1988) 45,
  136–7, 141
emotions, music as the language of
  the 28–9
enjoyment 21
enthusiasm 72, 149–50
epistemology 4, 19, 26–7, 39, 61–2,
  148
ethnic groups 57–8
evaluation *xiii*, 93–109: issues in
  93–7; use of term 93
examination results, publication of
  94; *see also* Grade examinations
experience, musical 8, 25–43, 48–9,
  63: memories of 105–6
extracurricular activities 4, 12,
  112–15, 148

faculty structure 63
failure, understanding of 106–17, 108
Fletcher, Peter 144
framing 60

Gabriel, C. 37
Gagne, Robert 69
Galin 27
Gamble, Tom 62
Gardner, Howard, *Frames of Mind*
  37–8, 39, 40, 58
GCE 87
GCSE
  London and East Anglian Group
  58–9; Music 20, 86, 87
generalists, in primary schools 70–1,
  89, 112, 128–9
genres, connections between musical
  58
Glover, Sarah 11
Glynne-Jones, Marjorie 146
government

intervention 93–4; links with
  140–1
Grade examinations 82, 83, 87–8
grammars of music *xi*, 31–2, 40, 51;
  see also deep structures
Grierson, David 53
Guildhall School of Music and
  Drama, *Music Performance and
  Communication Skills Project* 118–20
Guilford, J.P. 38, 122
Gulbenkian Foundation, *The Arts in
  Schools* 54, 62, 147

Hadow Report 135
Handbook of Suggestions for Teachers
  (1927) *ix*
Hargreaves, David 38, 117, 140
harmony 51
Hill, Kathryn 105–6
Hindemith, Paul 19, 30
Hirst, Paul *xi*, 30: 'Liberal Education
  and the Nature of Knowledge' 32
Hoggart, Richard 16
holiday music courses 137
Hornbrook, David, *Education in
  Drama xi*
Horton, John 124
Hungarian music schools 142

ideology 76, 142–5
image promotion 95, 113–14, 127
Incorporated Society of Musicians
  15, 140
independent schools 11, 111, 124
initial training 127–30
INSET provision 130
institutions, power structures and the
  curriculum 60–1
instrumental services 125
instrumental tuition 137: future in
  schools 131; selection for 37
instruments, arrangement for
  different 123
integration 59, 60–2

intelligence
  definitions 36; general 36; multiple
  x, 37–8, 148; musical 35–9:
  developmental models 80–1;
  psychometric tradition 36–7;
  structure of intellect model of
  38; verbal *ix–x*
'intended learning outcomes' 73
interest groups 140
interests, educating 56–7
interviews 97, 103–6

justification 1, 14–19, 20, 142–3

Kappelmeister role *xiii*, 122, 129
Keller, Hans 29
Kendell, Iain 96
Kitson 51
'know-how' 26
knowledge
  conceptual and perceptual 80;
  hierarchical organization of 79,
  89; music as a form of *x*, *xiii*, 4,
  19, 26–35; object and subject 17;
  propositional *ix–x*, 26, 32–3:
  limitations of 34–5
Kodály, Zoltán 53, 67, 71
Koestler, A. 122
Kwami, Robert 58

labelling 86
Langer, Suzanne *xi*, 19, 34–5, 40:
  Philosophy in a New Key 30
language
  functional 61–2; theories of music
  as 27–31, 35
language games 30–1
Lawton, Denis 57, 93, 126
learning
  teaching and 67–92; theories of
  130; transfer of 142–3
leisure education 15–16
Leng, Tee Sook 116
liberal education 10, 21, 32, 125, 132,
  135, 149

'line management' model 126
listening *xi*, 47
literacy, and thinking 53
Living Powers (Metcalfe) *ix*, *xi*, 11,
  35–6, 138, 147
Local Authority Initiatives 136
local education authorities, music
  services 135, 137, 140
London and East Anglian Group,
  GCSE 58–9
London Institute of Education 148
Lovelock 51

Macpherson 51
*Manhattanville Music Curriculum
  Program* 79–80
manipulative proficiency 81
meaning
  and emotion 28–9; public and
  language 28, 30; theories of
  27–31
melody writing 51
Metcalfe, Marian, *Living Powers ix*,
  xi, 11, 35–6, 138, 147
methods 49, 67
mind
  dualistic theory of 17; education as
  development of 19
model, teacher as 68–73
multicultural education, crude
  tokenism in 57–8
Murphy, William 51–2
music
  as an elegant pastime 11, 38; as a
  broad discipline 10, 149;
  ceremonial role 17–18; and
  combined arts programmes
  59–63; as language 27–31;
  optional at Key Stage 4 22, 45,
  136, 147; position of 136–8;
  social dimension of 121; status
  of 1, 95, 135–6
music centres 137
music curriculum 40, 45–66
music education

conceptions of *x*, 7–23;
progressive *x*, 3, 14, 17, 19; in
schools 11–13, 111–33; social,
personal and community aspects
115–22; traditional model *x*, 14,
19, 54–5; utilitarian model *x*,
16–17, 142–3, 150; writings on
139
Music Education Review (1977) 139–40
Music Education for Young Children
(Schools Council) 70, 96
Music from 5 to 16 (DES) 20, 88
music packages for non-specialist
teachers 70
*Music Performance and Communication
Skills Project*, Guildhall School of
Music and Drama 118–20
music profiles 85
*Music in the Secondary School
Curriculum* (Schools Council) 98,
127
music teachers
double role *xiii*, 112–15, 122–7; as
general
practitioners 59
musical activities 46–52: voluntary
111–12
musical thinking 35
Musical Times 88
musicianship 69, 113–14: training
128
musicological study 46

National Association for Education
in the Arts (NAEA) 61, 83–4, 141
National Curriculum
assumptions about view of
knowledge 139; music as a
foundation subject *xiii*, 11, 12,
131–2, 136; target orientation
68; weakness of 9
National Curriculum Council
(NCC) 141
Newman, Cardinal 11, 38
Newman, Christine 87

Newsom Report 15, 136
Norwood Report 135
Nuffield Foundation 95

objectives
models of curriculum 68, 73–8,
96–7; as part of common sense
teaching strategy 76; and
processes 73–8
objectivity
in assessment 83, 87; in classroom
research 102
Orff, Carl 67
organizational conditions and
constraints 146–8
outcomes, statements of 73–4

parents 137–8
participation, in extracurricular
activities 115–16
Paynter, John 8, 82, 98, 144: *Sound
and Silence* 144
pedagogy 130
'performance indicators' 94
performance *xi*, 47: as participation
76–7
performing-composing-listening
model 47, 58–9, 63
personal and social education (PSE)
12, 115–22
personality factor 102–3
Peters, Richard 19
PGCE courses 129, 131
Phenix, Philip 19
philosophy *xi*, 130
Piaget, Jean 17
pluralism 3, 57–8
Pointon, Malcolm 52–3
politics of the curriculum 140–1
popular music 56–7
positivism 19, 34
practice
identification of good 125–6;
theory and 9, 41, 142–5
presentations, public 112, 131

primary schools
  generalist teachers 70–1, 89,
    128–9; music in 51–2, 79; music
    teaching in 71–2, 112; special
    Hungarian music 142
Pring, Richard 61, 74
procedural principles 49, 50, 77
process model of curriculum 68,
  73–8
professional bodies 140–1
professional model of evaluation and
  development 97–101, 107
professionalism 9, 72, 101
progression 78–82
progressive ideals 3, 14, 47, 144
psychological model of education 17,
  39
public events 1, 95, 112–15
publicity for music and the arts 100
Pugh, Aelwyn 52
pubils' observations 103–5

qualitative aspects 64, 75, 77–8, 90
questionnaires 97

Rainbow, Bernarr 11, 144
Reid, Louis Arnaud xi, 17, 19, 33–5
relevance 55
Renshaw, Peter 118–20
research, integrated classroom 98,
  101–7
Research and Development 96–7
resources collections 137
Robinson, Gillian 84
Ross, Malcolm 17, 99, 144
Rousseau, Jean Jacques 47

Schafer, R. Murray 67
Schenker, 40
Scholes, Percy 12, 47
schools
  competition between 94–5, 114,
    130; links with local community
    120–1; music in 111–33
Schools Council 95–6

Arts and the Adolescent 8, 99–100;
  Inquiry 1 (1968) 136; Music
  Committee working party 136;
  *Music Education for Young
  Children* 70, 96; *Music in the
  Secondary School Curriculum* 98,
  127
Schools Music Association 140
Schwab, Joseph 9
Scrimshaw, Peter 30
Seashore, Carl 36
secondary schools, music in 73, 79,
  112
self-assessment 85
sequence, and progression 78–82
Sergeant, Desmond 87
Sexton, Stuart 137
Sharpe, Caroline 129
Shepherd, Frances 58
Shipman, M. 99
Shuter-Dyson, R. 37
Simpson, Kenneth 47
skill acquisition 52–4, 77–8, 127–8
Sloboda, John 38, 40
Small, Christopher 54–5, 144
social education 115–22
Somervell, Dr Arthur 73
specialist teachers 71–2, 89
Standard Assessment Tests (SATs)
  85
standards
  monitoring 94, 107; objective
    32–3, 87
star image 119
state schools 11, 124
Statham, Heathcote 87–8
Stenhouse, Lawrence 98, 106
Stravinsky, I. 31
subject matter 54–9
subjectivism 33
success 106, 108
Swanwick, Keith xi, 8–9, 47, 80,
  139–40: *A Basis for Music Education*
  20
symbolic field x, xi, 18, 30–1

targets 68, 78
Task Group on Assessment and
  Testing (TGAT) 84–5
Taylor, Dorothy 61, 69
Taylor, Michael 84–5
teacher appraisal 106, 125–7
teacher development, and curriculum
  development 98–9
teacher education, and music 127–30
teacher shortage 146; *see also* under-
  staffing
teacher survival 145
teacher training
  apprenticeship model 129–30;
    concurrent model 128;
    consecutive mode of 128; for
    music specialists 135
teachers
  and action research 102–3, 106–7;
    attitudes and behaviour 69; as
    authorities and models 68–73;
    enthusiasm and commitment 72,
    149–50; 'innovative fatigue' 9;
    isolation in schools 100; job
    specifications unreasonable
    124–5; non-specialist music
    70–1; professional status, and
    integration 61; reflection and
    self-criticism 97–8, 101, 149;
    role in music education 122–7;
    sharing of experiences 100–1;
    specialist music 71–2
teachers' centres 99–100
teaching
  conditions of 67–73; creative
    122–4; definition of 67; and
    learning 67–92; of music in the
    future 135–51; status and role
    113; 'to the test' 87–8
team work, in extracurricular music
  117
team-based teaching 146
test results, publication of 94
testing 86–7

theory
  and practice 7–8, 9, 99, 106,
    142–5; scepticism about 25
thinking
  aesthetic forms of 35, 148–9;
    literacy and 53; musical 35
Tillman, June 80
time, teachers' 108
time allocation 1, 146–7
Times Educational Supplement 127
tonality 28–9
Tovim, Atarah Ben 15
tradition, and innovation 2–3, 144
traditional approach to music 14, 47
traditions, epistemological 4, 26–7
transformation process 123–4
triangulation procedures 102, 103–5
tripartite system 135
Trotter, Yorke 27
Tyler, Ralph, *Basic Principles of
  Curriculum and Instruction* 73–4, 78

UK Council for Music Education
  and Training (UKCMET) 141
under-staffing 131
understanding, musical 2–3, 21,
  25–43, 145
utilitarianism 137, 150

values
  musical 19: Western 55; in teacher
    education 130;
  transmission of 68
virtuoso performer notion 82
vocationalism 16
voluntary musical activities 111–12
Vulliamy, Graham 55–6, 144

White, John 47–8
Williams, Raymond 140
Wills, Gillian 103–5
Witkin, Robert 17, 99, 144
Wittgenstein, Ludwig *xi*, 30, 62
workload, teachers' 124–5